ELEMENTS
OF A
HAUNTING

About the Authors

Brandon Alvis is the paranormal technician of the *Ghost Hunters* team. His twin passions for history and the paranormal led him to establish the American Paranormal Research Association (APRA). Brandon has investigated over two hundred public and private locations with APRA, many of which bear historical significance.

Investigations have included mental hospitals, prisons, well-known murder sites, cemeteries, and private homes, as well as more famous sites like Alcatraz Island, Preston Castle, and the South Pittsburgh Hospital.

As a natural skeptic, Brandon researches every location meticulously before he begins collecting evidence in an effort to make the study of the paranormal as credible as possible.

Mustafa Gatollari is the paranormal historian and site analyst of the *Ghost Hunters* team. For the last ten years, he has investigated alongside his New Jersey–based team, emphasizing the value of sincerity and legitimacy in his hunts. Mustafa has over eighty investigations under his belt. Although his focus is investigating private homes and helping ordinary people, he has also delved into everything from abandoned factories and shopping centers to a parking garage in Eastern Europe that had been built over a mass gravesite.

As a writer, Mustafa likes to approach an investigation the way an investigative journalist might approach a story—he not only enjoys conducting interviews with witnesses and digging into a property's public records, but he's also skilled in uncovering information quickly, which is an asset in any investigation under a tight schedule.

Praise for *Elements of a Haunting*

"These seasoned ghost hunters dispel some of the misconceptions and plain old flim-flam that plagues the field of paranormal research. They also offer a unique framework for classifying hauntings. This book is a welcome breath of fresh air."

—Richard Estep, author of *The Horrors of Fox Hollow Farm* and paranormal expert seen on *Paranormal 911* and *Haunted Hospitals*

"[Brandon and Mustafa] propose an interesting classification system that builds upon the shoulders of psychical research giants and that also raises questions about how ghost hunters should tackle cases ... Whether you pick up this book as a ghosthunter or, like me, as a scientist (who is a ghostbuster at heart!), you will find ... a book that will help you cross the boundary from the written word into the fascinating world of hauntings."

—Ciarán O'Keeffe PhD, MSc, PgCLTHE, BA, associate head of the School of Human and Social Sciences and associate professor of education and research at Buckinghamshire New University

"*Elements of a Haunting* is the first book I have ever encountered that truly dissects paranormal research as a credible scientific field. However, it is how Brandon Alvis and Mustafa Gatollari break down the humanity behind a haunting that sets this book apart."

—Malia Miglino, creator of *Macabre Mondays*

"These authors show that ... we can investigate the supernatural, acknowledge our humanity, and apply the principles of science rigorously at the same time."

—Jim Harold, host of *Jim Harold's Campfire* podcast and *The Paranormal* podcast

"Truly a milestone in the paranormal field. Not only does it contain detailed and thrilling stories that make the reader feel they are involved in the investigations themselves, it also establishes the connection between science and the paranormal ... An easy-to-follow guide for anyone looking to adopt these techniques in their own adventures."

—Lindsey Cennamo, *Lindsey Paranormal* YouTube channel

BRANDON ALVIS
MUSTAFA GATOLLARI

ELEMENTS
—— OF A ——
HAUNTING

CONNECTING HISTORY
WITH SCIENCE
TO UNCOVER THE
**GREATEST
GHOST STORIES
EVER TOLD**

Llewellyn Publications
Woodbury, Minnesota

FIRST EDITION
First Printing, 2022

Book design by Samantha Peterson
Cover design by Shannon McKuhen
"Holy Manor" cover image by Andrew Sciazko
Photos provided by the authors

Llewellyn Publications is a registered trademark of Llewellyn Worldwide Ltd.

Library of Congress Cataloging-in-Publication Data
Names: Alvis, Brandon, author. | Gatollari, Mustafa, author.
Title: Elements of a haunting : connecting history with science to uncover
    the greatest ghost stories ever told / Brandon Alvis, Mustafa Gatollari.
Description: First edition. | Woodbury, Minnesota : Llewellyn Publications,
    2022. | Includes bibliographical references.
Identifiers: LCCN 2021041658 (print) | LCCN 2021041659 (ebook) | ISBN
    9780738768229 | ISBN 9780738768489 (ebook)
Subjects: LCSH: Parapsychology—Investigation. | Ghosts.
Classification: LCC BF1029 .A48 2022 (print) | LCC BF1029 (ebook) | DDC
    133—dc23
LC record available at https://lccn.loc.gov/2021041658
LC ebook record available at https://lccn.loc.gov/2021041659

Llewellyn Publications
A Division of Llewellyn Worldwide Ltd.
2143 Wooddale Drive
Woodbury, MN 55125-2989
www.llewellyn.com
Printed in the United States of America

To David Vadim, for showing me how to fight for myself, and what to fight for. I love you.
To my wife, Mariam, and my children, Zack and Eva: when I'm doing my best, I'm fighting for you. I love you.
To Monday and Wednesday nights, and Friday afternoons: thank you.
To Distractify.com for always having my back.
—*Brandon Alvis*

To my brothers, Eric and Gary. Thank you for having such a huge impact on my life. To Taylor and my son Lucius, my love for you both will transcend this life into the next. To my parents, Kandy and Gary. Thank you for showing me how important life is on this plane of existence. To those that want answers to the ultimate question, does life extend beyond death.
—*Mustafa Gatollari*

CONTENTS

FOREWORD

Throughout history every civilization has created myths about supernatural entities that are capable of being observed by the living. Ghosts, shadow creatures, dark entities, souls, and lost spirits are believed to exist by people all around the world. Often such ethereal entities are mischief makers or downright evil, though occasionally these otherworldly entities are helpful, kind, or simply lost loved ones who have come for a visit to say final goodbyes or tell the grandchildren to behave themselves. Whether one believes in the afterlife or not, we are often entertained by such stories in books, television shows, and movies. And who among us doesn't enjoy a good ghost story around a campfire with friends and family, and of course s'mores? But do such entities actually exist? For more than a decade, reality TV series have entertained audiences, searching for proof of their existence, but unfortunately fall short of any solid proof that cannot be attributed to the human mind's tendency to find patterns, or the limitation of devices to detect anomalies. In science, we have strict rules of evidence, not because we are deniers, but because we know that real phenomena is measurable. If you use an instrument and detect a signal that is in the noise level that's within the sensitivity limits of the device, it's not really evidence of anything. The human mind is an amazing thing; we evolved to see patterns, which is why we see figures in clouds, or see animals in shadows when none exist. If we didn't have this ability, we would have perished long before developing tools or discovering fire. But the fact that irrefutable proof of the supernatural has not been found, doesn't mean that it cannot be found. When famed physicist Wolfgang Pauli introduced in 1930 an undetectable, invisible particle to explain energy nonconservation in nuclear decay, many considered it a fantasy. In fact, many called it a "ghost particle." Later, it would be named a neutrino, and eventually it would be detected and proven to exist. It's possible that we will discover solid evidence of supernatural entities one day. I, for one, would be thrilled at such a discovery. Like Brandon, I have suffered many losses early in life, including my father at age fourteen, and two brothers. Such loss builds a desire to know if there is something beyond the existence that we see. I was introduced to Brandon many years ago through a mutual friend, who was a member of American Paranormal Research Association (APRA). I joined this team as the resident scientist. Some might call me a skeptic, but all too often skeptics are driven by a desire to prove that ghosts don't exist. I find such people not only to be boors, but to be blinded by their nonbelief. As a scientist I don't seek to believe or disbelieve the supernatural, I seek to find evidence that would explain the phenomena that is so often observed around the world. That there is phenomena of various types is undeniable. Exactly what is that phenomena is what one needs to determine. Is it a trick of the mind? A chemical reaction to something in the environment? Ultralow sound frequencies? Magnetic anomalies that affect the human senses? Or truly supernatural entities? It is likely a combination of some of the above. Determining if one of those is supernatural requires the application of a scientific method, which to date has not really been applied. This is why I enjoy working with Brandon and the rest of the team at APRA, because they not only have a desire to apply the scientific method and to use devices that could actually detect signals above the noise level, but also understand that if supernatural entities exist, they might not all be the same. From different paths, we each reach the same conclusion that if you are to study the supernatural, a classification system is needed so you are not pooling every observation. Imagine going to Africa in search of a lion, and as you searched the forest and found evidence of animal footprints, scat, and heard animal sounds, you classified that all as proof of lions. If you did, you end up with no picture of a lion, as it is a mess of conflicting evidence. It would be absurd to do that. So why is it acceptable that most supernatural investigations just describe everything as evidence of a ghost or "haunting"? It's because they lack a good classification system. With such a system, you could begin to detail all the conditions around potential phenomena and perhaps find true evidence of various supernatural entities. In the book you are about to read, the authors put this principle into action. Whether you are a believer, a skeptic, or a scientist like me, I think you will enjoy the authors' approaches and the application of them to their own experiences/investigations. Now turn off all but one light, sit down with a cup of hot chocolate or a good scotch, and enjoy.

—Dr. Harry Kloor

INTRODUCTION

According to the Barna Research Group of Ventura, California, "eight out of ten Americans (81 percent) believe in an afterlife of some sort. Another 9 percent said life after death may exist, but they were not certain. Just one out of every ten adults (10 percent) contend that there is no form of life after one dies on earth."

Since my interest in the subject of life after death began, I have been into deep research about different beliefs and ideologies associated with investigating ghosts and hauntings. I began my research by going back in history to study the origins of phenomena. I started to look at case logs dating back to 1895, from researchers at the "Ghost Club" of London. To my surprise, well-known people like Irving Washington, Sir William Crookes, Lord Byron, Lewis Carroll, Titus Bull, and Charles Dickens had all investigated alleged hauntings.

After years of book research, I wanted to take that knowledge and adapt it to factual data collection in the field.

The opportunity to do just that presented itself when I was contacted by Pilgrim Media Group about a paranormal program they were producing. Years of working with my organization, American Paranormal Research Association (APRA), garnered the attention of the most prominent paranormal show ever created. A show called *Ghost Hunters*. When I first arrived in Los Angeles to screen test for the series, I was greeted by many paranormal investigators that were trying out for the team. It was all very chaotic until I met a guy named Mustafa Gatollari. One of the show's producers was pairing up team members to go in and investigate an allegedly haunted structure. Mustafa and I naturally gravitated to each other. Since that moment we have had one of the best friendships and working relationships that I've ever experienced.

Since meeting Mustafa in February of 2019 when we worked our first case for A&E's *Ghost Hunters*, we have actively been developing a classification system for ghosts and hauntings as a model for all paranormal investigators. Early on in our investigations with *Ghost Hunters* we started to recognize common patterns in haunted locations throughout the country. These patterns helped us implement the classification system to its fullest extent. The cases presented in this book will go into detail about the location's history, our investigation techniques, and how we use our research to explain factual data.

Mustafa and I will lay the foundation for a scientific approach to paranormal investigation. Not only will we introduce a classification system for ghosts and hauntings, we will also demonstrate the ethics, standards, methodology, protocol, and technology that led to this system. Join us as we connect history with science to uncover the elements of a haunting.

Brandon and Mustafa

— 1 —
IN THE BEGINNING, BY BRANDON ALVIS

Before we begin, Mustafa and I want to bring you into our world and show you how our journey into the paranormal began. Each of our stories are unique and from different walks of life. I will begin with how my life changed forever. Ghosts, hauntings, and the paranormal have been an interest of mine since a very young age. I can remember reading anything I could get my hands on that was related to ghost stories and encounters of a haunting. I was the type of kid that would walk by the local haunted house hoping to get a glimpse of said apparitions. Little did I know that this subject would transcend my life into a never-ending journey in search of the afterlife. It wasn't until 1995 that this interest would take on a new form. This was the first time in my life that I would truly conceive the concept of death and the thought of life after death.

September 8, 1995, after a short battle with cancer, my oldest brother passed away. This is the day that would change my life forever. I will never forget walking into my parents' house to my entire family sitting in the living room crying. Up to this point I didn't know what had happened, not even beginning to understand why my family was so melancholy. Thinking back I could feel the energy, the feeling of sadness hanging over the room like a dark cloud. At that moment I knew something was wrong, I just didn't understand what or why. My oldest sister called me over and sat me down on her lap. She hesitated a second before proceeding to tell me (her eight-year-old brother and the youngest of seven children) that our brother Eric had passed away. At first I didn't understand. How can you begin to tell an eight-year-old kid that he would never see his brother again? I began to cry; I couldn't understand what happened. One thing I did know, or rather I felt, was that something precious was lost that our family would never get back.

Eric was barely twenty-four years old at the time of his death. He left behind two young daughters, three brothers, three sisters, grandparents, a mother, and a father. As I write this, I am thirty-three years old. I remember looking up to my brother and thinking he was old, a grown man. Being now nine years older than my brother was at the time of his death, I understand that life has just begun, and Eric's life was cut so short. Everything changed for me; family and school was of disinterest to me. All I could think about was the concept of death and survival after death. I began to understand that there could possibly be something after life ends.

School wasn't always my favorite place to be. After the loss of my brother I was put into grieving therapy sessions with the school counselor; this made my school experience that much more undesirable. I was taken out of class to meet with the counselor every day for an entire year. A few months into the sessions I was joined by a girl a few years younger than me who had lost her father to a sudden heart attack. Even though I was only eight years old, and I was just beginning to grasp the concept of death, I knew she didn't understand what had happened. I knew she had absolutely no understanding or concept of life after death. Seeing this girl crying and questioning what happened to her father made me further question what happens after we die.

From 1995 to 2000, I spent the majority of my time after school at the cemetery where my brother was laid to rest. Every day my mother would pick me up from school and take me straight to the cemetery. On many occasions we would be there until sunset. Was this the best place for a grieving child trying to contemplate death and survival after death to spend a lot of time? Not sure. But I can say this: it started a fire inside me that will burn until my journey into the last great frontier ends. In the fall of 2001 my grandmother became ill and was hospitalized. After many years of being diabetic, her health problems had caught up with her. She was sent home on hospice to pass peacefully in the comfort of her home. This was the second time I experienced death. I was only fourteen and again the thought of a possible life after death came rushing back into my head.

It wasn't until 2004, at the age of seventeen, that my life would set out on a completely different course. My third-oldest brother, Gary, took his life on November 14, 2004. I was sitting at the kitchen table when the phone rang. It was my sister who immediately asked to speak with my father. I could tell from the sound of her voice that something wasn't right, that something terrible had happened. After dealing with the previous loss of my brother Eric and my grandmother, I felt something similar had taken place. My father was informed that Gary had died by suicide earlier that day. My brother Gary had battled with drug addiction over the years, and this would be a determining factor in his decision to take his own life. It wasn't until his funeral that the weight of everything that I had experienced would change my entire thought process about death and life after death.

I began reading everything I could about ghosts and hauntings, from such writers and researchers as Hans Holzer, Ed and Lorraine Warren, Sarah Wilson Estep, and many others. I wanted to make sure I had a proper understanding and knowledge of the subject prior to stepping out to conduct field research. After years of reading and researching, I was approached by a coworker who worked with me at the Buck Owens' Crystal Palace in Bakersfield, California. I was working as a stagehand and sound technician at the time. My coworker claimed that a friend owned a haunted house at the edge of town. At this point I was comfortable enough with my research that I volunteered to come out to the property to investigate the claims of ghostly activity.

The First Investigation: Wilkon's House

In the summer of 2005 I was connected through a coworker with a man named Jeff Wilkon, who claimed his property was experiencing ghostly phenomena. (Because this is a confidential case, I will use an alternate name for the client's anonymity.) When I first spoke with "Mr. Wilkon" he told me a local paranormal group had been conducting investigations of his abandoned farmhouse for a span of over three months. When I inquired about the phenomenon on his property, he invited me to attend the next investigation conducted by the local group. He was very reluctant to give me any information associated with his property and the phenomenon he believed was taking place.

On August 24, 2005, I drove twenty-five miles to an abandoned farmhouse located on the property of Mr. Jeff Wilkon. I arrived at the property at 7:00 p.m. The house was built in 1871 and was in terrible condition—no running water or power. I had to be extremely careful while walking throughout the house because of the many structural problems. Again I inquired about the property's history and said phenomenon to no avail. After a brief walk-through, the paranormal group arrived. Jeff introduced me to the leader and he immediately began to report the history of the location, starting with the deaths that had occurred on the property. According to the leader three deaths had taken place within this 1871 farmhouse, all under tragic circumstances. A five-year-old girl passed away of cancer in the 1930s, and a double murder had taken place in the basement and living room in the 1950s. I asked if they had any documentation of the deaths. Death records, police reports, burial records, anything to prove that these events had actually taken place in the house. He told me all of the information had come to them through their investigations. I was shocked and amazed that I was about to join an investigation with a team that had produced so many results in such a short period of time. I had so many questions. The excitement was unlike anything I had experienced. I was about to conduct my first field investigation in an actual haunted location!

At the time I had very little equipment: a small digital video camera with night vision capability, still photo camera, flashlight, and a digital voice recorder. I acquired the equipment while working as a stagehand and audio technician; I had no idea these devices would later be used on a paranormal investigation. After years of book research, this was my moment to actually investigate. I was asked to join the first group with three other investigators entering the dilapidated farmhouse. As we entered, the team leader instructed me on how the investigation would be conducted and that they would continue from where they left off from their previous session in the living room. Being that this was my first investigation, I wanted to observe as much as possible to learn everything I could about how a field investigation is conducted.

The interior of Wilkon's house.

I stood there quietly as the group started an Electronic Voice Phenomena (EVP) session in an attempt to reconnect with the spirits they previously encountered. It didn't take long before the group heard disembodied voices and saw shadows darting about the room. Two investigators had to be escorted out of the house after experiencing negative feelings. I have to admit, I was alarmed by the entire situation. This was my first attempt at field study and everything I'd ever read about negative entities was taking place before me. As I tried to remain logical, the psychic of the group began to verbally take on the spirit that entered the room. She started to speak in a different tone of voice and claimed the spirit had entered her body to use her as a conduit. It was then that I concluded that all the information about the deaths that occurred on the property was acquired through this psychic. I immediately began to calm my senses and think myself through the scenario. I never once heard the "voices" or saw the "shadows" they claimed to experience. As the psychic event continued, the present spirit claimed to be the killer from the 1960s. Yes, you read that correctly: the 1960s. I immediately said to the investigator next to me, "I thought the murders took place in the 1950s?" The investigator told me I would have to speak to the lead investigator. As soon as the group session ended, I approached the lead and asked him about the mix-up in dates. He said he had never mentioned a date associated with the murders, only the death of the young girl in the 1930s. I responded, "Yes, you said a double murder took place here in the basement and the living room in the 1950s." Responding defensively, he claimed again that I was mistaken and that he had not mentioned any dates. There would be one determining factor in this back and forth—the digital recorder I had used to record his explanation of the property's history. Despite our difference of opinions, I stuck around for the duration of the night to see how the remaining investigation was conducted.

The exterior of Wilkon's house.

Throughout the night it became a pattern—information kept changing from session to session. The age of the girl they said passed in the house changed from five to six and the story associated with the murders never remained consistent. I knew something about the group and the history they provided was suspicious. A few days after the investigation I contacted Mr. Wilkon to inform him of what I observed during the investigation. I told him about the mix-up in dates and that I had a recording of the information that was initially provided to me, as well as a recording of the information changing throughout the investigation. He began to tell me that he always found the information odd being that the property had been in his family for more than one hundred years and that he didn't know of any deaths that took place on the property. I asked him if it would be okay if I came out to investigate the farmhouse by myself. He was more than happy to accommodate.

At the time I was a guitar player in a metal band, and because I didn't know any other investigators I called my bandmates to accompany me to Wilkon's house for the investigation. Working for a live music venue and playing music was all I knew, so I didn't have ample investigative equipment yet. Instead I utilized some of our band's recording gear along with my digital video night vision camera. On September 4, 2005, my bandmates and I arrived at the abandoned Wilkon's farmhouse to conduct our first investigation. I immediately set up a condenser microphone connected to a USB interface that ran into recording software on a laptop. This setup was far more powerful than any handheld digital recorder. I was able to hear every slight noise throughout the entire house. My knowledge as a sound technician would help me excel in collecting Electronic Voice Phenomena. I continued the setup with my infrared night vision camera in the kitchen, which filmed the living room where one of the deaths allegedly took place.

Once everything was set up, I asked everyone to reassemble outside where I had a base camp set up to review the live audio that was being recorded in the house. I wanted to make sure the environment was as controlled as possible. I decided we would take turns monitoring the live audio and allowing the house to settle to see what noises were natural. After a few hours of silence, a strange noise was picked up on the microphone. The more I listened the more it became clear that it was the sound of footsteps. As these sounds continued, a deep voice could be heard accompanying the phantom footsteps. I was completely baffled at what was being recorded. I was listening to a live recording of an empty room that sounded as if a man were walking around talking to himself. After the sounds ceased, two of my bandmates and I entered the house to see if there was someone inside. The house was completely empty. Luckily we had a camera recording in the room where the sounds were captured. Little did I know that a significant piece of data was collected to support the audible phenomenon we had just recorded. After three more hours of silence, I decided to break down the equipment and head home to analyze the audio and video recordings. I was so full of adrenaline that I began reviewing as soon as I got home. After hours of listening, I finally reached the point in the recording where the footsteps and deep voice were collected. I listened to this eight-second clip over and over to try to make sense of what was happening in the recording. After reviewing the unexplained voice, it was clear I needed to consult a professional with proper knowledge of audio recordings. Could there be a natural explanation for this unaccounted-for voice? I decided to move on to the digital video camera that was set up in the kitchen to monitor the living room. The over six-foot-tall shadow figure I saw on the recording would change everything I knew about the paranormal. Unfortunately I was never able to investigate the Wilkon's house again. The property was sold, and the house was demolished a short time later. Little did I know this investigation would propel me to start my own paranormal organization that would one day lead me to being on the hit TV show *Ghost Hunters*.

Shadow person captured at
Wilkon's house in September 2005.

In the Beginning, by Mustafa Gatollari

I was always chickenshit. My cousins and brother loved playing hide-and-seek in the dark. I hated it. My father and older brother would often call me into a room to watch *Ninja Turtles*, and when I entered the room, they'd turn on the TV and Freddy Krueger would pop on the screen, knives on his hand and that charred face, sharp grin, and awful, awful voice. I'd scream, running out of the room with my hands over my ears, eyes closed, bumping into furniture and wall corners, straight into my mother's arms as I questioned her decision to have children with such an awful man.

Which is why, when I became the go-to person for my family and friends and then their friends to investigate their paranormal claims, they'd scoff at first.

My interest in the field began like every haunted house horror movie. Except the cast was a superstitious working-class Albanian family of eight with peasant origins. The peasant part is important later.

There was something off about our sprawling, three-story home in New City, New York. It's something that I, my siblings, my parents, and anyone who spent an extended amount of time in it would attest to.

We moved in when I was four years old. It was the biggest house my family had ever lived in, and still is to this day. In retrospect, it's head-shakingly predictable: We left our congested apartments in Lodi, New Jersey, after my father got the house for a steal. For some reason (it was haunted), no one had wanted to buy it for five years despite the excellent school ratings and size of the home and yard.

When you're a kid, sometimes you're too naive or dumb to be scared. Which is probably why I didn't react like I should have after walking into the main living room after finishing our inaugural dinner in the kitchen of our new home.

I remember standing in my white and neon-pink surf T-shirt (I didn't surf back then, still don't today) wondering why every box we had carefully brought in from our station wagon, unpacked, and splayed out in different parts of the living room were all somehow pushed into a single corner. Neatly packed.

I was looking at the indents in the carpet from where the boxes had sat for hours when my mother came up and put her hand on my shoulder. Then she gasped and started speaking Albanian to my father, a sign I knew something serious had just happened.

She and my father continued their Eastern European whispers behind hushed doors. They recited verses from the Quaran through the night, along with my grandfather and grandmother.

Looking back, it's easy to want to grab my father by the shoulders, violently shake him, and say, "GET THE HELL OUT OF THE HOUSE!" like an overly excited theater-goer who can't believe that ditz just walked into the cabin alone. At night. With a dead battery in her car.

Now, I understand why my dad chose to ignore it. He had dropped a fat down payment on the home. He had dreamed of a suburban life for us, tired of cramming the whole family into a couple of small apartments that he and his father worked eighty hours a week at factories and diners to eventually own. Our large family was there to stay despite it all and I somehow, still, was unafraid.

I was even unafraid when my brother and I heard thumps and cracks beneath us in the middle of the night. "Can you hear that?" I said. Even in the darkness I could see how wide-eyed and excited my older brother was. We slipped out of our beds and crept out of our bedroom on the third floor, following the sound down our large central stairway. It grew louder and louder as we passed under the chandelier until we made it to the kitchen, where the sound was the loudest. We stood there and I held my brother's hand; he didn't shrug me off like he usually did.

I rubbed my eyes when I finally saw the cause of the noise: our kitchen cabinets were opening and closing by themselves. We looked at each other, smiled, and uttered a "whooooaaaaa" that Keanu Reeves would approve of. My mother must've thought the two of us were up to some middle-of-the-night mischief, because she joined us soon after. I remember how her face changed from, "You little assholes!" to a steely, "Get upstairs and go to sleep."

Breakfast the following morning contained more whispered Albanian between my mother and father, while my brother and I giggled, not believing we were surrounded by magic.

The sightings in the house were another thing that should have terrified me, but instead I was fascinated. It was strange. You couldn't get me on a roller coaster when my father took us to the Keansburg, New Jersey, amusement park. I screamed and cried so hard on the Loop-O-Plane that the tattooed ride operator finally flicked his cigarette and ended the ride. I couldn't look at the Predator's face as he laughed maniacally in some South American rainforest and the countdown for his atomic bomb went off. But watching my toys come to life in the middle of the night as my brother slept across from me felt like a fascinating dream. I'd be paralyzed, but still not frightened enough to want to leave. When my mother swore to my father the face of Cruella de Vil on a completed Disney puzzle turned her head to look at her, I spent hours putting the damn thing back together, only to stare at it for hours, hoping to see the same thing.

I'd often venture into the garage to catch a glimpse of the man my brother said was untying his shoelaces, and then "tied them around his neck, Mommy, and jumped." The thought of seeing the man didn't scare me. Neither did the "fire babies" my younger brother and sister spoke of who flew above my mother's bed.

As the years progressed, our family's luck worsened. My father lost work. My mother fell ill, diagnosed with asthma and an ever-worsening case of hypothyroidism. While those probably had natural explanations, the day of my grandfather's first stroke, however, still sends chills up and down my spine.

As my mother tells the story (and I recall as a seven-year-old): she was home alone with me, my younger brother, and my younger sister. My grandmother and grandfather left to see my aunt Flora in Maywood, New Jersey. It was about forty-five minutes away from our new haunted house.

My mother thought they had been out of the house for some time, so she was surprised to see my grandfather walking down the main stairwell. I, too, remember kissing my grandma and grandpa goodbye. I would've gone with them but wanted to stay home because my older brother was at a friend's house, which meant I could finally play some SEGA without him ripping the controller out of my hands.

Thinking he was gone already, my mother called out to my grandfather, but he never looked back. He only went down the stairs and turned right into the living room. She never saw his face. Bewildered, she asked me to go and check in the living room for him. I sighed, hit pause, and went down the stairs into the living room. No one was there. I couldn't find him. So Mom called Flora, telling her that my grandparents just left. I could hear Flora was confused on the other end. (Albanians are loud talkers.). They had already been there ten minutes when my mother called. So who the heck did my mother see walk down the stairs? Was she seeing things? Maybe.

Three to four hours later, my grandfather collapsed in the backyard of Flora's home. He was admitted to the hospital; the doctors told us he had a stroke. I remember seeing him, tubes pushed into his nostrils and other parts of his body under a white blanket. My mother caught me looking at her as she quietly spoke with Flora, both of us making the connection at the same time. My grandfather survived and was back to normal after some rehabilitation, but as far as I know, no one ever informed him of the doppelgänger incident.

Our family's fortunes worsened, and it wasn't long before my father began speaking of Jinn. In the Quaran, it's said that God (Allah) has two primary creations: men and Jinn. I started hearing all the old-country stories of these beings and the mischief they caused.

Stealing farmers' horses for their personal wedding celebrations. Jinn kidnapping people, possessing others, and causing misery and personal misfortune for entire families.

It was around that time I started having horrifying nightmares. Bedtime was a death sentence. I'd wake up every thirty minutes to an hour, unable to shake off the feeling that a Jinn was waiting close by for me to be at my most vulnerable to either possess me or take me away to some dark dimension where I'd never again be able to hear my mother's soothing voice or get into terribly one-sided fights with my mean-ass older brother.

After a few years of living in our huge, haunted house, my uncle fell on hard times. So he, his wife, and their five kids moved in with us. The bottom floor of our home—what we called "the basement"—was enormous. It had a full bathroom, its own kitchen, a living room, and three other rooms they converted into bedrooms. There were fifteen of us living in the house, and every day we played, fought, and ate together. We'd still hear strange noises. Items were misplaced, cabinets and dressers that were closed would open by themselves, and the nightmares, although consistent, only came in bouts. Then, after being filled to the brim with people for so long, the activity stopped.

As I grew older, I began to wonder if it was Jinn after all. My father attributed the disappearance of the activity to his renewed devotion to Islam. For years he attempted to do business with the Saudi royal family, who loved keeping him around as a court jester of sorts: he was Muslim but looked like an ancillary character from a Scorsese gangster flick. He spoke multiple languages, so they could count on him to accurately translate the Italian or French or Polish or Czech from their various dealings, none of which he got a taste of.

So my father finally severed ties with the royal family and did what Eastern Europeans do best: he started a construction business. The realtors took pity on us, giving us ample time to leave so they could display the home during open houses. My mom always made sure it was clean for them, which was a daunting task for a woman taking care of two senior citizens and four insane kids.

The construction business took off and we moved back into the apartments in Lodi. Anytime a member of my family or my friends in the private Islamic school my father enrolled me in began to talk of Jinn or anything supernatural, my blood boiled. Otherworldly entities, as far as I was concerned, weren't the cause of my family's misfortune, a series of idiotic business decisions on my father's part was. The growing tension between my mother and father wasn't because of the devil and his minions. The fact that she had entered into what was pretty much an arranged marriage at the age of seventeen was.

When my father, again, started getting delusions of international travel and business grandeur, leaving his construction business aside, our finances suffered once more. He was quick to attribute this to bad luck, which is when I decided to prove to him and the rest of my family once and for all that our home in New City was not haunted. There was no misfortune attributed to a curse, no Jinn attached to our family, just plain old human stupidity.

I began to look into everything about the property. I called up the county records office. I learned about the land it was built on. I didn't eat lunch for years, saving up the measly two dollars I'd get every day for lunch to pay for my brother's gas to drive me to visit my old hometown multiple times. When he was unavailable, I'd spend hours riding the bus, studying at stations, and doing my homework on dusty seats.

The more I looked into that home, the more I discovered that there was nothing to suggest our home was beleaguered by Jinn. It was built by a successful businessman and was one of the first houses in the area to have central air and a jacuzzi. It was an architectural wonder, the product of someone who lived in a wealthy area and wanted to flaunt his success. A man who mysteriously went missing.

Wait, what?

I needed to know the person who built this home. Would he be evil? Would he look like a villain from an early '80s fantasy flick? Would he have a goatee and sharp features and long fingernails?

But I never got any answers, which was my answer. All I knew was that he had mysteriously disappeared, and the bank had taken over the house. After asking longtime neighbors in the area about our house's previous owner, I was told he had fallen into a deep depression, and two separate people told me they believed he had taken his own life.

It was maddening to not have any further answers on the house that ruined my family, and that madness turned into a nagging, persistent itch. I knew there was something inexplicable going on in that house, but it could've been a Jinn or a demon. Could it have been a man dealing with some trauma he decided he'd had enough of? Did it go away once he saw not one, but two families struggling and trying their damndest to thrive in spite of not knowing if they were going to have a home the next month?

Although all my siblings and I went to an Islamic school, my extended family came to me as the go-to Holy Man as I was traditionally more devout. I prayed five times a day. I'd memorize and recite a ton of Quaran and assiduously worked on my classical Arabic pronunciation. I'd visit Islamic conventions, sleep in the masjid during Ramadan, and my fervor carried on into my undergrad years in college. Since stories of my haunted house were well known, close family members and friends asked me to come and bless their homes or tell them if anything evil was going on there.

The little time I had free from classes or the part-time jobs I worked, I'd visit them, mainly to provide practical advice for solving their problems. I'd pray in their homes, I'd give them verses from the holy book to recite, and I'd record our sessions. I took every case as an investigation, learning as much about the property as I could. They thought I was looking for demons, but what I was really doing was trying to discover whether or not some residual spirit or energy was left there from a person who lived there previously, as I suspected was the case in my childhood home.

In many cases, it turned out that the cause of their problems wasn't ghosts or evil spirits. They didn't have a hex; they just hated their job. The evil eye didn't curse their relationship; they just caved into their parents' wishes and had a shitty marriage. They weren't lethargic and depressed all of the time because a Jinn made them that way; they just ate like crap and never exercised.

It was around this time that *Ghost Hunters* first came on the air and I saw what a methodical, professional approach to paranormal investigation looked like, so I started incorporating those methodologies into my own cases. Family members started having their friends reach out and soon I was traveling to all parts of New Jersey, New York, Connecticut, Pennsylvania, and Delaware to help members of the Albanian-Muslim community with their Jinn woes, almost all of them home cases.

I enlisted the help of my younger brother and a friend of his who was obsessed with ghost hunting and collecting evidence of the paranormal. We pooled together our resources to buy equipment: video and audio recorders and back-up hard drives (which weren't cheap back then). My primary focus was always to ensure that the living had the best lives possible. I viewed the investigations as therapy.

I was always, always, always very skeptical when it came to the paranormal, and my dogged pursuit of those questions was to disprove. I didn't want people to blame their problems on supernatural forces as my family did. But the more I investigated, the more fascinated I became with my past experiences, because, like anyone who's had a paranormal experience will say, "I know what I saw." But I didn't believe, or I just *couldn't* believe that ghosts were real.

And even after years of helping others and coming across some truly inexplicable experiences, feelings, and evidence that I couldn't comprehend (an EVP my former team member showed me that I unknowingly captured in an abandoned parking garage in Serbia that ended up being a mass grave site from the Kosovo War still baffles me to this day), before joining *Ghost Hunters*, I was very much a skeptic.

However, after working on these cases with Brandon and the rest of the team, while I still approach every investigation as a skeptic in methodology and practice, I've just seen, documented, and witnessed too many things to rule out the possibility that paranormal occurrences are very much real.

And we have compelling proof they are.

— 2 —
GHOST SCIENCE

In 2006 I founded American Paranormal Research Association (APRA), a scientific paranormal research team organized to investigate historical locations throughout the United States. APRA's goal is to open the eyes of the scientific community in order to understand the unexplainable and to obtain proof that life after death is a great possibility. Our mission is to collect hard, irrefutable paranormal evidence to present to the public and scientific community.

It wasn't until 2011 that my entire perspective and approach to investigating the paranormal changed. One of the lead investigators for APRA introduced me to a scientist by the name of Dr. Harry Kloor. Dr. Kloor is one of the only people in history to receive two PhDs simultaneously: one in physics and the other in chemistry. APRA and I immediately started working with Dr. Kloor on our research. Since APRA's inception, I have looked to move the field forward; I always believed that science and proper protocol would be the way to do it. Bringing Dr. Kloor on board completely changed everything we thought we knew about scientific principle.

Brandon looking through newspaper archives.

In 2014 Dr. Kloor, along with APRA, was featured on an episode of the Science Channel TV show *The Unexplained Files*. Because of our work implementing science into paranormal research, we were the subject for the episode titled "Shadow People." This was one of the first times audiences throughout the world were able to see a world-renowned scientist work with a group of paranormal investigators. Our work on the show instantly became controversial, not only in the paranormal community, but in the scientific community as well.

Dr. Harry Kloor and Brandon at X Prize Foundation.

Out of the three episodes we filmed for the Science Channel, only one of them hit the airwaves. Our investigation of a former reform school called Preston Castle was the subject of the aired episode. According to some of the staff and various paranormal investigators, a new menacing phenomenon was taking place within the castle: shadow people. Not only did we want to investigate the paranormal possibility of the said phenomenon, but we also wanted to see if there was a rational or scientific explanation for these experiences. Dr. Kloor devised an experiment to test the theory that people visiting the castle were being influenced by fear pheromones. In the wild, hunted animals release a fear pheromone to alert the rest of their herd that a predator is nearby. Dr. Kloor wanted to test each participant's cortisol levels after spending a night within the castle. Were certain people being affected by others' fear pheromones?

The test was inconclusive. What made this significant was that this proven scientific test could not account as a natural explanation for the said phenomena.

It was this particular experiment that caused a lot of controversy within the paranormal field. Social media and paranormal websites were abuzz with different takes on the experiment. Multiple science-related publications also spoke about our experiment and the episode. I had wanted to take my research in a scientific direction since 2006, and after working with Dr. Kloor for a number of years, I was ready to take the idea of ghosts and hauntings to the next level. There has been a lot of different research over the years, but there is one aspect the field has lacked: a classification system for the different types of ghosts and hauntings. With this very book, you are going to see years' worth of field investigations and research put into practice. We will look at the various formulas that create a haunting to connect science with history to tell the greatest ghost stories ever told.

Equipment

Digital Audio Recorder: In our research we use digital audio recorders in an attempt to document Electronic Voice Phenomena, also known as EVP. These devices are crucial to help determine if we are experiencing unexplained audible or recorded vocal activity.

Binaural Microphones: The binaural microphone greatly aids our search for Audible Voice Phenomena. This device not only mimics human hearing, it gives us superhuman listening capabilities.

Ambisonic Microphones: This device is mainly used in virtual reality, but we have adapted the ambisonic microphone to work in paranormal research. Not only does the ambisonic give us 360 degrees of recording capability, but it can also help us determine where an unexplained voice is generating from.

Data Logger (EDI+): The EDI+ is what I refer to as the Swiss Army knife of all paranormal equipment. Environmental conditions play a huge role in the formula of a haunting. This device gives our research an all-in-one tool to record temperature, humidity, pressure, electromagnetic frequencies, and vibration.

TriField TF2 EMF Meter: Electromagnetic frequencies (EMFs) have always been a huge part of paranormal research. The TriField TF2 EMF Meter aids us in detecting man-made and natural EMF. This helps us rule out all contamination before concluding there is a paranormal cause.

4K Infrared Cameras: Night vision is a staple in the paranormal community. Investigating locations at night can be extremely helpful when controlling an environment and trying to cut down on contamination. This 4K technology gives us higher resolution to monitor a location.

FLIR Thermal Imaging Camera: Any time we seek natural explanations to paranormal encounters, the thermal imaging camera plays a major role. Not only will this device help us look for natural occurrences, but it also detects hot and cold spots that cannot always be explained.

Electron Multiplying Camera: Photons have been a huge interest in our research of ghosts and hauntings. The Electron Multiplying Camera (EMCCD) has given us a way to see if photons are being generated in haunted locations.

Body Camera: These devices are typically used in law enforcement, but we have adapted them to document our investigations from a point of view not typically seen. Documenting our personal experiences is a must to present these encounters as data rather than a story.

Motion Detectors: Mainly used in home security, motion detection aids our research when unexplained movements take place. These devices have helped us direct our attention to areas of a building that would typically be overlooked.

Classification of Ghosts and Hauntings

The Class of Haunting system is a collection of terminology I started to develop in 2007 after years of field and book research. It contains terminology that's been used within the paranormal field dating back to case logs from 1895. My goal was to adapt the entire field's thoughts and theories into one simple structure. This classification system is how our team refers to different types of ghosts and hauntings and as we continue our research more classes will be added. Our goal for the classification system is to determine the type of haunting and what the source may be. Documenting the environmental data is crucial in our search for answers and correlating the environment with paranormal activity will help us determine a haunting. We may better understand what type of phenomena is occurring and why it might be taking place using this system.

Each of the five classes includes established terminology to describe types of phenomena. Some of the phenomena may fit into multiple classes (e.g., a guilt-ridden entity is classified as a "class two helping entity," but may also be malevolent (class four)).

Class One: Haunting Apparitions

A figure or figures that are seen in the same place on a series of different occasions by one or more people.[1]

- **Emotional Attachment:** A spirit that is attached to a location or object that was dear to them in life.[2]

- **Grey Ladies:** The ghosts of women who are said to have died violently for the sake of love or through the heartless actions of a family member or loved one. They frequently appear grey, but they can also appear white, black, or brown.[3]

- **Innocence Ghost:** Traditionally, the spirit of a woman who is seduced and then deserted by her lover, only to die in a consequence of the act (e.g., in childbirth or by suicide in grief over the illicit affair).[4]

Class Two: Helping Entities

These entities will appear in the event of helping someone or warning them of possible danger.[5]

- **Familial Apparitions/Hauntings:** Ghostly apparitions said to be associated with a particular family.[6]

---

1. Emily Peach, *Things That Go Bump in The Night: How to Investigate and Challenge Ghostly Experiences* (Thorsons Pub, 1991).

2. Hazel M. Denning, *True Hauntings: Spirits with a Purpose* (St. Paul: Llewellyn Publications, 1996).

3. Theresa Cheung, *The Element Encyclopedia of Ghosts and Hauntings: The Ultimate A-Z of Spirits, Mysteries and the Paranormal* (Harper Element, 2010).

4. Cheung, *The Element Encyclopedia of Ghosts and Hauntings.*

5. Peach, *Things That Go Bump in the Night.*

6. Cheung, *The Element Encyclopedia of Ghosts and Hauntings.*

- **Guilt-Ridden Entities:** Spirits that haunt a location because of a previous act in life they cannot forget.[7]
- **Crisis Apparition:** A spirit tied to the location where they passed that is trying to reveal a message about their life and/or death.[8]

Class Three: Restless Spirits

When a person suffers a traumatic/sudden death, leaving them with unfinished business, this can create a restless spirit.

- **Bound by Loved Ones:** A spirit that remains to stay with a loved one or is looking for a loved one.[9]
- **Suicide Apparition:** The spirit of someone that has taken their own life and regrets the act.[10]
- **Murdered Apparition:** The spirit of a person that was murdered by the hand of another.

Class Four: Malevolent Entities[11]

A spirit that is intent on inflicting harm to others.

- **Green Ladies:** Phantom apparitions of ladies dressed in green gowns that often act as heralds of misfortune or death.[12]

---

7. Denning, *True Hauntings*.

8. Peach, *Things That Go Bump in The Night*.

9. Denning, *True Hauntings*.

10. Peach, *Things That Go Bump in The Night*.

11. Peach, *Things That Go Bump in The Night*.

12. Cheung, *The Element Encyclopedia of Ghosts and Hauntings*.

- **Hag:** An apparition reported to resemble an ugly old woman with tangled hair, rotting teeth, a hooked nose, mad eyes, and claw-like fingers. The hag is also related to the mara (from which the word nightmare is derived), a demon that likes to attack and abuse humans at night.[13]
- **Radiant Boys:** Ghosts of boys who have been murdered. They are believed to be an omen of bad luck or death.

Class Five: Pseudo Hauntings

This class is designated for unknown haunting groups.

- **Elementals:** Manifestations of the four elements: water, air, fire, and earth. Elementals are usually associated with the practice of magic.[14]

Now that we've broken down each class and how it may pertain to the elements of hauntings, this class system will be used to describe each case you will read about in this book. We will cover cases that were featured on the A&E reboot of *Ghost Hunters*, as well as cases dating back to 2006 that were conducted by the American Paranormal Research Association. With this new approach, we hope to further paranormal research by giving it a structure and protocol that may help lead us out of the shadow of pseudoscience.

---

13. Cheung, *The Element Encyclopedia of Ghosts and Hauntings*.

14. Cheung, *The Element Encyclopedia of Ghosts and Hauntings*.

— 3 —
ETHICS, PROTOCOLS, AND STANDARDS

There are currently no experts in the paranormal field, but with the advancement of technology and science, we as a field can move forward in our thinking and standards. If we want to be taken seriously by the public and scientific community, we have to put in place certain ethics, standards, and protocols. In this chapter we will lay out the protocol we follow to find the formula for hauntings. Following this format and data collection platform will help utilize the classification system. When we go to a zoo, we don't say that we saw animals. We break it down by species. This classification system will help bring similar structure and terminology to a field that is currently shrouded in pseudoscience.

In order for us to advance as a field, we should collect factual data and empirical evidence from around the world. We can encourage people to use sections and templates from our research to log data for themselves. This would include where they live, which would allow us to host a world database for phenomena that can be cross-referenced. In turn we could identify any observable patterns and the formula for hauntings. We could then start to categorize the types of history associated with various phenomena.

Mustafa: There's a dearth of methodology in the paranormal field and this is a serious problem. Many people hide under the guise of ParaUNITY in order to enlist others to participate in their self-delusion and fortify bubbles of not having their evidence challenged. It's impossible to be an expert in the field, and I don't consider myself one.

However, there are ways to scientifically document the correlation between environmental changes and inexplicable occurrences, and we believe this is a huge step in seriously subjecting paranormal finds to scrutiny. By utilizing tech adapted from other industries with their own respective experts who specialize in said technology, we can then ascertain what caused the strange, documented activity and categorize these anomalies as practically explained aberrations, or legitimate paranormal phenomenon.

Like Brandon always says, "If it ain't normal, it's paranormal." By utilizing a strict investigative protocol that mitigates false positives and puts the investigator in a position where they can easily ascertain what's "normal," then all we're left with is evidence that is worth analyzing even further.

Data Collection

Preparing for an investigation is very crucial. Not only do you need to have an understanding of the property, but you need to be very aware of all the environmental conditions associated with the site. You need to be familiar with the layouts, the blueprints, and the history. You must be informed as much as possible in order to draw a conclusion in a case. Always approach the investigation from an unbiased standpoint. Collecting factual data and empirical evidence is key. Every investigator needs to collect data in order to have an understanding of what's happening in a haunted location. So, go in and remain unbiased, calm, grounded, and logical. Find the natural explanation for said phenomena and go from there. The data you need to gather in order to make a sufficient case log includes:

- History associated with a location
- Geography of a location
- Notable wildlife
- Proximity to water
- Date
- Time
- Moon phase
- Humidity
- Temperature
- Barometric pressure
- Wind speed
- EMF / electromagnetic frequencies (man-made and natural)
- Video / audio data
- How many people have observed the phenomena

• Gender and age of observers

• Age of the building

• History of the land

• Folklore from the area both indigenous and local (modern)

Mustafa: Factor in everything, and I mean everything, when conducting an investigation because you may find interesting correlations down the line. A great example of this is the changes in barometric pressure we encountered in our investigations. Why are there correlations between Electronic Voice Phenomena (EVP) and visual anomalies with pressure? Hell if we know, but we've ascertained that this is an irregularity worth exploring further and implementing as part of future experiments. Will creating a vacuum in a specific area spur on more strange activity, or does the ghost or strange phenomenon incite this change in pressure? Another example is the correlation between geography/building materials or any minerals present causing these environmental changes. There's a long-standing theory that limestone is known to have retentive properties. In our season one, episode nine ("Home for the Haunting") case in Willimantic, Connecticut, we documented what appeared to be residual activity on the staircase on four separate occasions. All three Data Loggers registered pressure changes, sequentially, in the same area where the client reported audible footsteps, which we heard during the course of our own investigation. Was this phenomenon related to the limestone foundation in that particular home? What other cases can we relate this to that had similar activity in a location with lime stone in the earth or in the building itself?

Ethics

"In 1842, Julius Robert Mayer discovered the Law of Conservation of Energy. In its most compact form, it is now called the First Law of Thermodynamics: energy is neither created nor destroyed. In 1907, Albert Einstein announced his discovery of the equation $E = mc^2$ and, as a consequence, the two laws above were merged into the Law of Conservation of Mass-Energy: the total amount of mass and energy in the universe is constant."[15] I have always been a believer in this theory: energy is neither created nor destroyed. If we believe that the energy that our body is made up of can't be destroyed, where does that energy go? Does it retain consciousness? If it does, and these energies that we communicate with are in fact the consciousness of people, respect is key in any investigation. I believe we should always be aware of the manners and etiquette of the location and time period we investigate. This will give us better understanding and cooperation of the possible entities we interact with. Are ghosts, in fact, disembodied people?

Historical events play a huge role in the formula of hauntings. As a field we have to hold ourselves accountable for factual historical research. If we cannot back up an event with documentation, we cannot utilize this information for research purposes. Our field is plagued by misinformation and urban legends that are taken as fact. Our case logs should contain factual historical documents that will help us understand why there is phenomena taking place at each location.

---

15. Antoine Lavoisier, "The Conservation of Mass Energy," Chem Team, https://www.chemteam.info/Equations/Conserv-of-Mass.html.

Mustafa: I've met a lot of investigators who said they are skeptics, but if you really didn't believe in the possibility of ghosts or paranormal spectacles, there's a good chance you're not going to get involved in this field. Skepticism is something I wrestle with on a daily basis and it's why I am so entranced whenever I come across a phenomenon I am unable to readily explain.

After working on so many cases, I've personally come to believe that there are truly supernatural happenings worth looking into further. However, even if one isn't a skeptic, it's important to approach each case from a dubious mindset, which can be difficult to accomplish when one obtains footage they believe is otherworldly. So how does one separate fact from fiction?

A good rule of thumb: if you're participating in mental gymnastics to prove what you captured is paranormal while ignoring basic questions that poke holes in your theory that something is paranormal, you're working the wrong way. When fellow team member Daryl Marston and I encountered what we believed was a large shadow figure ambling down the hallway of Fort Stanton's Hospital (season two, episode three, "Proof of Afterlife") a floor above where Brandon captured a fascinating apparition on the EMCCD camera, we were ecstatic. However, upon attempting to re-create that figure the following night of our investigation, we saw that the window down the hall cast a similar effect. Yes, our Data Logger was registering pressure changes out of nowhere after hours of inactivity at the exact same time this episode occurred, but we didn't feel right showing this footage to

the client. As much as we believed that what we encoun
tered was something truly special.

I'm going to pat myself on the back here. I pride myself on not giving into my feelings that what we captured was evidence of the paranormal, and even more
shallowly, trying to force a ghost theory because it'd
make for good TV. I firmly believe, as Brandon does,
that it's more important, and frankly more entertain-
ing, to showcase actual investigative protocols to our
viewers than to push the idea that everything's a super-
normal entity.

Protocol

Baseline readings are crucial in our research. Any time we enter
a location, we must gather baseline data readings of the entire
property. Date, time, moon phase, humidity, temperature, barometric pressure, wind speed, EMF/electromagnetic frequencies
(man-made and natural). If we are not monitoring these readings
throughout the investigation, we are not gathering the proper
information for our research. All equipment should be running
simultaneously and documented via a timecode to ensure that we
are in full understanding of our environmental conditions at all
times. Audio and visual control devices must be recording from the
moment of stepping onto a property. Recording audio and video
throughout the entire investigation process will help maintain
proper documentation via the timecode.

Standards

The quality of our equipment and technology is going to make or
break our advancements in the field. Many of the gadgets made

specifically for paranormal research are flawed and riddled with false positives. We have to open up our evidence and data to third-party scrutiny. Any time Electronic Voice Phenomena (EVP) is collected, the audio data should be tested through spectrum analysis to see if the EVP in question is a stray radio frequency, cell phone frequency, or the result of any man-made contamination. The same goes for visual evidence. We should always have visual evidence tested by a third-party video engineer to ensure that we are not dealing with a camera artifact or natural occurrence. Science should be our friend, not the big bad wolf of the paranormal field.

Investigation

We will now break down how we conduct our investigations from start to finish. As the field currently stands, there is not a right or wrong way to conduct paranormal research. We hope that this can one day become a guideline for all paranormal researchers and investigators.

- Initial client and eyewitness meetings (Take copious notes and audio and video recordings; have the client fill out a questionnaire; psychological testing; check for medication, drug, or alcohol abuse.)

- Historical research (Death records, Sanborn fire insurance maps, blueprints, period photos, land deeds/grants, newspaper articles.)

- Location walk through (Be sure to look at every square foot of the property. Where is the phenomena taking place?)

- Baseline readings (Collect all data prior to the investigation. Continue to monitor that data from the first baseline reading until the moment you break down the equipment. All data recordings should run simultaneously on a timecode.)

- Communication (Approach the possible entities with respect and knowledge of their life and time period. Explain the technology and why you are there. Attempt to record EVP and document any visual anomalies. Make sure that all of your control devices are running at all times. Take audio, visual, and environmental readings.)

- Break down/media management (Be sure to collect all media and secure it in a safe place. Designate a team member that will be in charge of all your data, including SD cards, DVR systems, and hard drives. All data and investigation information should be dated and timestamped.)

- Analysis (Designate certain team members to analyze all data information. If you find something that you believe to be unexplainable, contact a third party from a technical industry to help you understand the data. This person should be an expert in the field of the data in question. How does the data match the timecode? What are the environmental conditions associated with the phenomena? Is there a recognizable pattern?)

- Final client meeting (Reveal all information collected in your investigation. Be sure to be as thorough as possible with that information. Provide copies of all data and documents associated with the case. Closure for the client is key.)

Once the final client meeting has concluded and you have provided your data and conclusion, be sure to remain in contact with the client for all of their needs to understand the phenomena going forward.

Mustafa: Here's a theory of mine when it comes to investigation that's made all the difference in my cases: while evidence comes first and foremost, it's extremely important to gauge your own character when entering an investigation. Not you as a Ghost Hunter, not you trying to act like a professional in front of your team or a camera, not you taunting any potential entities to get them to talk to you, but you as an individual, as a person. Can you honestly generate interest in the location you're investigating? If you can, this could be the difference between possibly communicating with an entity or having a completely flat night where nothing happens except you talking to yourself with nothing to show for it. While those nights occur more often than not, if you aren't at least fighting to enjoy yourself by having an honest reaction to your surroundings and dealing with those feelings, or lack thereof, then why even investigate? This will sound philosophical, but it's a personal code I strive to live by: give everything of yourself in any situation and you'll never regret it. This includes teeing off on the elephant in the room. I'll never forget expressing this sentiment to Brandon when we investigated a slave shack in Thibodeaux, Louisiana, on St. Joseph's Plantation (*Ghost Hunters*, season one, episode eleven, "Blood on the Bayou"). It felt almost offensive to attempt to sympathize with any entity who could be present, as much as we tried. We weren't documenting any activity on our equipment until I began to question why we were there in the first place. Instead I addressed the biggest question looming over our heads: how could we ever sympathize? I expressed that it would be impossible for Brandon and me to ever truly know what a slave or laborer on that plantation would have endured in their lifetime, and even though they didn't have a say in the matter, and even though it was against their will, I told them their work shaped our country for the better. And we thanked them for that.

While Brandon was reviewing audio for that particular leg of the investigation, he excitedly called me to his room. After I gave my spiel, you can hear, clear as day on the recording, a woman saying, "Thank you." And that was that.

So never shy away from honest expression in trying to make a situation better, no matter what that situation is. Theoretically, entities are people and if you treat them as such, they will respond in kind.

— 4 —
TECHNOLOGY AND
THE PARANORMAL

Brandon: Since 2006 I have made it my mission to advance the field and to push paranormal research into a true science. With the rapid advancements in technology, this gives us a clear path to step out of the shadow of pseudoscience. When I first began field research, I started to see the many common mistakes within the paranormal field. This prompted me to implement the scientific method and to assemble a panel of experts from various technical industries. Many of the gadgets invented specifically for paranormal research are riddled with flawed theories and false positives. There are no experts in the paranormal field as of today. Yet, there are many investigators that look at the scientific method as the big bad wolf. In my sixteen years of active field research, I started to compile data to develop the classification system for ghosts and hauntings. The data and techniques used to implement this system will be laid out in this chapter.

False Positives Are Not Proof

Mustafa: If I spent the entire day telling my son that there was an invisible monster in his house that loved eating two things: jam and kids' feet, he'd probably express his disbelief, most likely after telling me what a mean father I was for attempting to scare him without provocation. But if later on while he was in the bathroom brushing his teeth I put an empty jar of jam near his bedroom slippers, that might get him thinking there's something strange going on.

Bad paranormal tech works in a similar way. It's predicated on our belief that there's something more to the world of empirical thought. Then a narrative is constructed as to what a device is capable of documenting, and then that narrative is combined with the spooky stories of a particular location. When that amalgamation is subjected to a field investigation and a piece of garage tech goes off, some people will use that as definitive proof that there's a ghost, spirit, demon, Jinn, balrog, etc. among them.

When you find yourself omitting valid questions and challenges to a paranormal encounter and are heavily relying on technology that crumbles in the face of scientific scrutiny, then you're just looking to be entertained by suspending disbelief. What you're then doing is LARP-ing as a paranormal investigator rather than actually investigating the paranormal.

Theory and Protocol

It'd be impossible to issue a list of end-all-be-all equipment that paranormal investigators should never deviate from. The field is an ever-growing one, and any shred of progress that's made is an exciting opportunity to introduce new technology that'll help push a field forward that's been held back by ghost-loving snake-oil salesmen.

However, there are some sound theories and practices that should be adhered to when one is investigating, which extends to how devices are selected for a scenario.

As many strange experiences as we've had, our data gathering and documentation cannot be skewed towards any bias. To remove the emotional aspect of a haunting experience, we start by focusing on environmental changes.

What is an environment's habitat? There are countless folks who ghost hunt at an abandoned building at night and jump at a shadow that suddenly passes ... only to discover later that it was a quiet car that passed under a streetlight outside. Get to know the ins and outs of one's location: the temperature, moisture levels, appliances that may be inside an area, cracks in the wall where a draft can enter, etc. Familiarizing yourself with your surroundings as much as possible will help you get to the bottom of whether or not something is paranormal. Besides, if you're fond of spooky experiences, then we promise you, there's nothing uncannier than doing everything in your power to vet an occurrence, only to come up short with any logical explanation.

The reason why we document changes in the environment is thus: if we begin to notice aberrations in these environmental factors—a sudden drop or spike in temperature, barometric pressure, or a blast of EMF that wildly deviates from the area's norm—that's cause for interest and prompts some actionable questions that beg to be answered. What prompted the sudden environmental change? What can I do to re-create it? Can I re-create it?

That's when you can dig further and try to find a natural explanation. Does the spooky occurrence happen at regular intervals? If so, try to find the root of this cause and replicate it. If you can't, then dig into your video and audio recordings of the investigation to try and understand what caused it.

If you can't re-create the environmental changes you're documenting, and they happen to correlate with other unexplained activity, then that's cause for even more interest. Do you notice that whenever an inexplicable event occurs there are other environmental changes that preclude or follow it? Or do they happen at more or less the same time? This is why following a strict investigation protocol is so important, as is documenting phenomenon on multiple devices.

We've experienced this on several occasions in our investigations and we've noticed some truly game-changing correlations, one of which is a sudden shift in barometric pressure.

> **Brandon:** Environmental conditions associated with hauntings can lead to very significant data. Once we start to recognize patterns within environmental changes, especially when unexplained phenomena occur, we as a field can start to analyze and catalog that data. Similar to a Farmer's Almanac, we have to start taking these environmental conditions into account. Pressure, temperature, humidity, electromagnetic frequencies (EMF), vibration, moon phase, tide charts. All of these factors will lead to a better understanding of the formula of a haunting.

When it comes to theory and protocol within the paranormal field, I believe it is crucial for the field to adopt a code of ethics, protocol, and methodology that can help every investigator and organization stay true to true empirical evidence and data. I also believe that the field has to open up its evidence to third-party scrutiny. Consulting professionals from other technical industries will separate natural phenomena from unexplained phenomena.

Data Logger

Since we're on the topic of environmental changes, specifically pressure, there are a variety of different tools that can be adopted from other industries, including agriculture, meteorology, construction, electrical engineering, geology, etc., that can be implemented for paranormal investigating. No, they don't need to have the word phantasm in their name or depict an intimidating devil figure on the box; they just need to reliably register changes in environmental conditions.

The EDI+ Data Loggers that we utilize in many of our investigations effectively package a barometer, motion detector, thermometer, EMF or tri-field meter, and a humidity gauge in one compact package with the added benefit of charting and graphing that data. While they're fast becoming a favorite tool of paranormal investigators because of their convenience and ease of use, there's nothing ghostly about the product: it merely detects fluctuations in environmental conditions.

There are a variety of different tools one can use to chart the data that's collected on this tool as well. WeGhostHunt.com has a free visualizer that is capable of reading the comma-separated values, but one could easily enter the data into MS Excel, Google Sheets, or other free tools like ones offered by Analog Flavor. All you need to do is find a piece of software that reads .CSV files and you're good to go. The best part is, you don't need that much storage space to save the files, so even lower-capacity SD cards (1 GB or 2 GB) will be just fine in most investigative scenarios.

Photon Events and Pressure

In several of our investigations, we have noticed that there is almost always a significant relationship between strange activity and sharp changes in barometric pressure. It's one thing to have an experience while investigating: a sudden chill or to feel that something has moved past or through you. But to then document simultaneous changes in environmental conditions like a sudden drop or spike in pressure while correlating a photon (light) phenomenon validates one's experience.

With the introduction of the EMCCD camera into our investigations, we have documented multiple photon events that almost always correlate with changes in pressure, and the nature of these events vary from case to case and location to location. However, they always share one constant: the phenomenon can never be re-created. They seem to have their own energy sources. The only thing that comes close to these documented episodes are the creation of other photon events, like when we lit a match in Clifton, Arizona, during the season two premiere of A&E's *Ghost Hunters:* "Terror Town."

While investigating claims in the town's boarding house of a strange mist passing between two rooms, the Electron Multiplying Camera caught these wispy anomalies flying through the air, as if it was a scene from *Poltergeist*. Upon further inspection of the camera and giving it to an expert who's familiar with the device, we ascertained that what we captured were photons that had their own energy sources. We captured insects flying on the camera and they looked nothing like these energy sources. Shining lights in front of the camera both inside the room and outside from the windows proved futile as well. We created a storm of dust in front of the camera, but again, nothing. The only event that came close to the phenomenon we documented was the generation of heat and energy that came from lighting a match.

So why are photon events so important? Because, according to Sir Roger Penrose, one of the most brilliant mathematicians ever, they don't have any mass. Since they don't have any mass and travel at the speed of light, that means, essentially, time is irrelevant for a photon. Since they don't measure time, the moment of a photon's creation is immediately followed by infinity.

Ghosts or Time Warps?

This is where things get a bit heady. There is an interesting theory that's still in its nascent stages but is nonetheless worth considering. And that's the idea that the ghosts we theoretically investigate in all cases aren't necessarily spirits roaming the planet after death. There could be a case made that paranormal investigators aren't always interacting with individuals who have passed away but are rather speaking with these entities at a specific moment in time. This is why the correlations between our findings with photon events and pressure changes are so intriguing.

We've documented on several instances that these light anomalies captured with the EMCCD camera almost always go hand in hand with significant aberrations in barometric pressure levels. So in theory this could mean that living beings who have died can manifest themselves as an energy source that is not only a type of light that can be captured by Electron Multiplying Cameras, but that can also alter its environment in some way, usually, in our cases, as pressure and in some cases, EMF.

But what if we aren't interacting with someone who has passed on, but are rather communicating with them via a rip in time? What if we're actually speaking to someone via a time loop of sorts?

Again, this is all theory, but there are several paranormal occurrences that lend itself to this theory. Oftentimes, individuals speak to a doppelgänger effect on their cases; investigators will swear they've seen their partners, colleagues, or even themselves during the course of their work. Is this an entity imitating them or their colleague? Or did they happen to perceive an occurrence that's actually a rip in time? Time, after all, is relative as per Albert Einstein's theory of special relativity. Space.com states that Einstein "determined that the laws of physics are the same for all non-accelerating observers, and that the speed of light in a vacuum was independent of the motion of all observers."[16] This means that our traditional understanding of physics, especially when it comes to objects that travel at the speed of light (i.e., this phenomenon that we're documenting), have special rules when it comes to their relationships with time.

So are we talking about time travel? Or rather, communicating with individuals through some type of time traveling cosmic telephone of sorts? It's a heady concept that's difficult to grasp, and we're only beginning to consider its implications ourselves, but there's some very intriguing studies about black holes that could help us to better understand what we've documented regarding

---

16. Nola Taylor Redd, "Einstein's Theory of General Relativity," Space.com, November 7, 2017, https://www.space.com/17661-theory-general-relativity .html.

photon events and pressure changes. *Express UK* published an article about black holes potentially holding the key to time travel. In the article, researcher Atharva Palshetkar broke down a black hole's role in time travel as such:

> *"If someone was supposed to see you falling down a black hole, he would see you going slower and slower, taking weeks, years and even decades, until you reach a point where light can't escape the black hole's event horizon. The viewer then just sees a spaceship stuck at the event horizon until it gets red shifted and it gradually disappears. Meanwhile, while you enter the black hole everything you see outside will begin to speed up outside. Your family, kids, grandkids, hundreds of generations will rise and fall in just matters of minutes and hours."* [17]

In short, our perception of time during these strange occurrences is altered.

Back to Sir Roger Penrose: his discussion of photons came up during his visit to the *Joe Rogan Experience* podcast, where he offered up his thoughts on black holes. Penrose has said that the last things to exist in a black hole will be "photons," [18] and these huge masses of matter packed into a relatively small space consequently have

---

17. Sean Martin. "Black holes may be the key to time travel and make 'billions of years pass in minutes,'" *Express UK*, May 24, 2020, https://www.express .co.uk/news/science/1178555/black-hole-time-travel-time-dilation-how-to -time-travel-possible-black-hole-earth.

18. Joe Rogan, "1216: Sir Roger Penrose," December 18, 2018, *The Joe Rogan Experience,* podcast on Podchaser, https://www.podchaser.com/podcasts /the-joe-rogan-experience-10829/episodes/1216-sir-roger-penrose-34876792.

extremely strong gravitational pulls. So strong that not even light can escape them.

So what do photon events have to do with black holes, the concept of time, and pressure? NASA has offered up some absolutely mind-blowing information on black holes, and these cosmic phenomenon encapsulate the very nature of life, rebirth, and the grandest scale imaginable:

> *"Recent discoveries offer some tantalizing evidence that black holes have a dramatic influence on the neighborhoods around them—emitting powerful gamma ray bursts, devouring nearby stars, and spurring the growth of new stars in some areas while stalling it in others."*[19]

For the purposes of our research, however, it's this bit about a black hole's effect on time that calls into question our entire understanding of the paranormal field:

> *"As the surface of the star nears an imaginary surface called the 'event horizon,' time on the star slows relative to the time kept by observers far away. When the surface reaches the event horizon, time stands still, and the star can collapse no more—it is a frozen collapsing object."*[20]

---

19. "Black Holes," NASA Science, https://science.nasa.gov/astrophysics/focus-areas/black-holes.

20. "Black Holes."

Black holes have long been a focal point of our most brilliant minds' study of humanity's concept of time; Kip Thorne's 1994 book, *Black Holes and Time Warps*,[21] is one such popular example.

A recent *Yale News*[22] article also referred to an *Astrophysical Journal*[23] study that proposes pressure is a key ingredient to the formulation and growth of black holes. These gobs of tightly packed matter "feast" on pressure and grow at an accelerated rate.

While we can't begin to pretend to understand the nuances and complexities of black holes, photon events, and their relationships to pressure and the nature of our perception of time itself, we can attest that nearly every single one of the paranormal occurrences we've documented on our EMCCD (Electron Multiplying Camera) have, again, also had strong correlation to changes in pressure.

If time doesn't exist in a black hole, and photon events do not abide by the regular rules of time as we know it, and time effectively "stands still" while a black hole is "engorging" itself and expanding in one of its highly pressurized feasts, then are we actually capturing evidence of a ghost? Or are we peering into a momentary time warp and connecting with an individual or event from another time period?

Or are ghosts actually residual energy from our bodies that we converted to photons after we die? After all, matter is neither created nor destroyed according to the law of conservation of mass

21. Kip S. Thorne, *Black Holes and Time Warps* (New York: W. W. Norton & Company, 1994).

22. Jim Shelton, "Under pressure, black holes feast," YaleNews, May 22, 2020, https://news.yale.edu/2020/05/22/under-pressure-black-holes-feast.

23. Angelo Ricarte, "A Link between Ram Pressure Stripping and Active Galactic Nuclei," *Astrophysical Journal Letters* 895, no. 1 (2020).

by Antoine Lavoisier, and neither is energy. And thanks to Einstein, we've arrived at the theory that the total amount of mass and energy in the universe is constant. So could it be that the ghosts we're capturing evidence of are really just a transmutation of energy from the past or even future?

Again, we don't know the answers to these questions, but we do believe that when it pertains to the paranormal, we've helped cement a lead for further investigations and experiments that'll help us better understand the nature of seemingly inexplicable phenomenon. It has less to do with demons, angels, spirits, souls, and heaven and hell, and more to do with these constantly recurring correlations between pressure changes and photon events. All we can do is diligently document our findings along with the environmental conditions that surround them and establish correlations.

— 5 —
THE GREY LADY

It's difficult to not be immediately impressed by the Athenaeum and its surrounding area situated between Renaissance Place and Lockerbie Square in Indianapolis. Our investigation took place on some of the hottest days of the year, but even though every instinct prompted us to rush inside, each member of the team, along with cast and crew members, took a few moments to soak it in. The architecture, simply put, was beautiful. Embedded stone facade columns, immutable brown brick, the Athenaeum dripped with history. Plucking it out of context and out of time, it could easily be the residence of an eccentric count with a dark secret in a Gothic novel.

The Grey Lady at the Athenaeum

- Indianapolis, Indiana. Investigated in 2019 on A&E's *Ghost Hunters*. (Season one, episode seven, "Dancing with the Dead.")

Claims

- Shadow figures were spotted in the Athenaeum's restaurant.

- Shadow figures were reported walking throughout the building's various hallways.

- Multiple performers in the Athenaeum's theater have claimed to see an old couple dancing. Upon approaching the couple, they disappear.

- A former trainer for the YMCA, located in the Athenaeum, saw a woman in white floating above the ground in the workout area.

- On a visit to the Athenaeum, author Nicole Kobrowski saw the figure of a woman enter a conference room and then vanish.

- Lights turn off and on in administration offices by themselves.

- Voices audibly heard in the theater when no one is present.

- Scraping sounds of items being moved in the theater were heard. Upon inspection, nothing was moved and there were no marks on the theater's wooden floor.

- Feelings of dread and negativity were reported by employees in a storage unit above the theater, nicknamed Grandma's Attic.

History

It's easy to overlook how important the Athenaeum was to Indianapolis' growing immigrant German population when construction began in 1893. Originally called Das Deutsche Haus (the German House), it opened its doors in 1898 primarily as a physical fitness center for local gymnasts, or *Turners*. For many German American communities during this time period, socializing and exercise often went hand in hand, so it was normal for social clubs to be called *Turnverein*, which roughly translates to gymnast club. Interestingly enough, one of America's most notable fiction writers has a connection with the center. Das Deutsche Haus was designed by architects Arthur Bohn and Bernard Vonnegut.

If you're wondering if Bernard Vonnegut was related to Kurt Vonnegut Jr., then you'd be right: Bernard is Kurt's grandfather. Bernard developed a close personal and working relationship with Arthur in Germany. The two men worked as teachers in an industrial training school and then opened their own architectural firm. They were tasked with the enormous responsibility of designing and building what was quite possibly the most significant German cultural center in America and the most significant undertaking of their architectural careers. It's evident from Das Deutsche Haus's construction that the two men were intent on not only making a statement, but also creating a timeless structure that would serve the needs of their community. And they did. Originally including a "gymnasium, locker rooms, meeting rooms, auditorium, ballroom, restaurant, and a beer garden for the Socialer Turnverein Aktien Gesellschaft," [24] the building was a lofty design project for any designer, especially at the end of the 1800s. To put it simply, Vonnegut and Bohn absolutely killed it.

Das Deutsche Haus was so well received that it opened up other opportunities for the two men, who went on to design several other buildings in Indianapolis. They are largely responsible for the distinct atmosphere and aesthetic of the Athenaeum's surrounding area,

---

24. Robert W. Smith and Dorothy A. Nicholson, "VONNEGUT AND BOHN ARCHITECTURAL RENDERINGS, 1896, 1911," Indiana History, December 2007, https://indianahistory.org/wp-content/uploads/vonnegut-and-bohn-architectural-renderings-1896.pdf.

dictated by the construction of their formidably designed and persistent projects that are standing tall today.

For new US citizens who hopped off the boat, leaving their native Germany behind and suddenly finding themselves in a whole new world, Vonnegut and Bohn's Das Deutsche Haus was a bastion of hope and comfort. Not only was it a redoubtable structure that elicited awe from first glance, but it also provided immigrants with the familiarities of their homeland along with an established community of experienced individuals who could assist them in acclimating to their new lives in America. This was a vital emotional component for our work on this case. As investigators, we don't always look for the dark and gloomy backstories associated with a property. We've found intense personal connections, both negative and positive, can tie individuals to a location. Given that the Athenaeum meant so much to so many different people, in many instances being the first place they felt at home in America, it makes sense that they'd persist there, theoretically, after they passed, much like the Athenaeum, itself, persists.

World War I changed everything for Das Deutsche Haus. Anti-German sentiments began fomenting in the area and in an attempt to get ahead of any discriminatory attacks against the building and its members, board members changed the name to the Athenaeum. However, programs in the community center began suffering. Fewer and fewer members attended meetings and social gatherings in an attempt to downplay their German heritage and fly under the radar until the war was over and it was acceptable to be from Deutschland again.

Today, the name Das Deutsche Haus is emblazoned in front of the Athenaeum, an homage to its profound origins. It was made a nationally recognized historic landmark in 2016 and is currently directed by Craig Mince, who contacted *Ghost Hunters* to get to the bottom of the hauntings in this historic location.

The Murder of Dr. Helene Elise Hermine Knabe

(Note: Nicole Kobrowski's book, *She Sleeps Well: The Extraordinary Life and Murder of Dr. Helene Elise Hermine Knabe,*[25] is an excellent resource for more background information on this fascinating woman. A big thanks to Nicole for meeting with us, as many of the details of the doctor's case were used for our *Ghost Hunters* investigation and further background on her case in this section.)

To be a woman in the early 1900s was difficult enough, but being a woman who not only worked, but thrived in a predominantly male-dominated field was like living on the hardest difficulty setting if life were a video game. That's exactly what Dr. Knabe did and a quick glimpse at her life reveals that the woman, to put it bluntly, was a badass. She immigrated from Germany to Indianapolis in 1896 with dreams of becoming a doctor and immediately got to work. Possessing an extraordinary mind and a steel will, Dr. Knabe immediately studied to become fluent in reading, writing, and speaking English. She attended classes at Butler University and made positive impressions on everyone she came into contact with. It was evident that she was not only a no-nonsense hard worker when it came to her studies, but that she was extremely intelligent. She was soon granted admission into the Medical College of Indiana and became only one of two women to graduate from the institution in 1904.

It didn't take long for her to secure gainful employment as an instructor at the Athenaeum and a medical researcher. When she

---

25. Nicole R. Kobrowski, *She Sleeps Well* (Westfield, Indiana: Unseenpress.com, 2016).

wasn't conducting experiments and recording the results of her studies, often collaborating with male doctors in the field who respected her work ethic and medical acumen, she was teaching health courses at the Athenaeum to children and teenagers. While she prepared and shared a variety of different biological lectures with her students, she was somewhat of a controversial figure as she covered sex education as well.

Class instruction on sex still ruffles feathers to this day. The fact that a woman in the early 1900s, in a conservative community, was talking about sex to young and inquiring minds caused the doctor to be the topic of many hushed and scandalous conversations. Nevertheless, she was known as a pillar of the community and frequented the Athenaeum, and not just for work; she attended many of the social events when she wasn't publishing medical journals and cutting up cadavers for her research. The cadavers were provided to her by Alonzo M. Ragsdale, an undertaker and friend of Dr. William B. Craig, who was a dean of the Indian Veterinary College. The relationship Dr. Knabe had with these two men would take a dark and tragic turn.

A Frivolous Cover-Up

On October 24, 1911, Dr. Knabe was found dead in her Delaware Flats apartment located a few blocks from the beloved Athenaeum she visited multiple times a week. Her passing came as a shock, but even more outrageous was the claim from Police Chief Martin Hyland that Dr. Knabe had died by suicide. Why would someone who was so cherished by her community and created so many endearing relationships with those around her, who was making such unprecedented advancements in the medical field *as*

a female doctor, and in many cases earning more money and acco-
lades than her male counterparts, kill herself?

Then there was the nature of her alleged suicide: she was found
with her throat slit from "ear to ear."[26] There were two cuts administered by someone who obviously knew what they were doing:
the first slice had missed her carotid artery but was deep enough
to cause Dr. Knabe to choke on her own blood. The second had
lightly penetrated the artery and entered her spine. Chief Hyland
offered that because she was 5'6 and 150 pounds, she would've
been strong enough to fend off any attackers. That's it. That's the
only evidence provided for the suicide ruling. Never mind the fact
that there was no blood on Dr. Knabe's hands. Never mind that
the window to her apartment was found open. Or that a bloody
fingerprint was ignored (even though the science of fingerprinting
was still fairly new). It didn't help matters when Detective William
Burns, who was once dubbed "America's Sherlock Holmes" said
her death was a suicide. The only trouble was, he didn't actually
conduct an investigation. He just read reports in the newspapers.

Local newspapers covered the brutal death and featured many
interviews from those who knew the doctor. They highlighted a
great number of those who personally knew the doctor as a skilled
teacher, ardent researcher, and wonderful person. She also had
many detractors, with some who more or less stated that she got
what she deserved. Those negative comments were more than
likely influenced by rumors surrounding Dr. Knabe's sexuality: she
was an unmarried woman working a man's job, so, of course she

---

26. Nicole Kobrowski, "Dr. Helene Knabe: Revictimized in Death," Indiana History Blog, July 30, 2018, https://blog.history.in.gov/dr-knabe-revictimized
-in-death/.

must be a lesbian. It didn't help matters that she was teaching children about intercourse, either.

The coverage of her death included these rumors regarding her love life, along with untrue accusations of a deteriorating financial situation. It seemed that the ghastly suicide of Dr. Knabe that reeked of foul play would be ultimately forgotten, and the truth behind her death would be forever hidden.

Until coroner Dr. Charles O. Durham ruled there was no way in heaven, earth, and hell that Helene could have administered both cuts to her own neck and would obstinately not budge from reporting his findings. Unnoticed or unreported by the police were defensive wounds on Dr. Knabe's arms, which strongly suggested she was attacked in the middle of the night. The evidence gathered by Dr. Durham emboldened an outraged community of Dr. Knabe's friends she had so happily served. A group of female doctors took it upon themselves to find her killer and hired private detective Harry Webster. They pooled together their resources and raised money from locals who happily donated to the cause in the hopes that a third party could get to the bottom of this gruesome case. Detective Webster, after learning the particulars of the doctor's alleged suicide and pursuing the case for several months, stayed on for months after the money ran out, donating his time as a pro bono PI.

The anger and faith of the community, along with Detective Webster's sound investigative work and the personal convictions of coroner Durham ultimately paid off. One year and three months after Dr. Helene Knabe's death, two men were indicted: Dr. William B. Craig and Alonzo Ragsdale.

A Crime of Passion, Jealousy, and Revenge Unravels

The prosecution offered that the prominent slash found on Dr. Knabe's body would be one that Dr. Craig was very familiar with performing being the dean of students at a veterinary college and a financial stakeholder of the same institution. A sheep's cut was administered from ear to ear on her neck. It's a cut that butchers are familiar with and use to avoid major arteries, which curbs blood spurting. Theoretically, whoever implemented such a cut would do so intentionally to curb the amount of blood that ended up on their hands.

Here's the proposed motive as to why Craig wanted Helene dead: it was rumored that the two of them were engaged and that she may have been pregnant, something Dr. Craig passionately denied in court. However, evidence gathered by Detective Webster loudly contradicted Dr. Craig's denials: in a letter to a friend, Dr. Knabe mentioned she was getting married. A receipt for a costly dress commissioned by Dr. Knabe was also found in her possession. It's highly unlikely she'd pay for a gown if it wasn't for a special occasion, since she was a well-known seamstress who made clothes for herself and others.

It also didn't help Dr. Craig's case that in Dr. Knabe's same letter, she referenced the man she was betrothed to had an "unforgivable temper," and there were several eyewitness accounts recalling arguments between the two of them and instances where Dr. Craig flew off the handle at the mention of Helene's name. A colleague at work testified to an ongoing dispute between the two doctors. Dr. Knabe wanted to move her lecture time with Dr. Craig and went to the board to get approval. When Dr. Craig was asked by the colleague for his answer on the matter, he screamed, "Oh fuck! Tell her to go to hell!" His own housekeeper recalls an argument between the two of them in Dr. Craig's home, hearing Dr. Knabe say, "But you can continue to practice and so can I!"

Dr. Craig's motive congealed in court even more when the evidence against his friend, Alonzo Ragsdale, came to light. Alonzo was also a business partner of Dr. Knabe; as an undertaker he'd provide her with cadavers for experimental purposes. She would joke that after her death, she'd be happy to continue to do business with him by giving him her corpse. He was indicted as a co-conspirator in her death by assisting to paint her murder as a suicide. It was believed he stole the kimono Dr. Knabe was murdered in and had it washed to remove blood stains. In addition to being an undertaker, Alonzo was also an estate executor, who had wrongfully painted Dr. Knabe's financial status as a desperate one.

Dr. Knabe had several revenue streams as a teacher, medical researcher and practitioner, seamstress, and artist. Coroner Durham, likely incensed at the blatant foul play that took place in the investigation of Dr. Knabe's death, had taken it upon himself to delve deeper into Helene's finances and discovered that she was making some $150 a month. By 2020 standards, that resulted in a purchasing power of approximately $4,000, as per the US Department of Labor's inflation calculator.[27] To put it into even greater perspective, rent in NYC, arguably the most expensive place to live in America at the time, averaged $10 a week. Which means that Dr. Knabe, who rented a modest one-bedroom apartment in Indianapolis, would've had at least $110 to spend on food, clothing, and entertainment. She was no pauper as Alonzo had alleged.

A series of attacks against her character were presented in court by the defense and many echoed sentiments already expressed by

---

27. "CPI Inflation Calculator," U.S. Bureau of Labor Statistics, https://www.bls.gov/data/inflation_calculator.htm.

her detractors in newspapers: she was a thirty-five-year-old unmarried woman, rumored to be a lesbian (which was absolutely scandalous at the time), valued work over family, and had money troubles. The latter was ultimately proven false. Stories leading up to the trial also left out the fact that the good doctor sent money to an uncle who was physically unable to work.

Unfortunately, the standing of Dr. Craig and Alonzo in the community ultimately seemed too much for their indictments to materialize into convictions. Although Dr. Knabe's suicide was officially ruled a murder, the key witnesses who had signed affidavits incriminating William didn't testify in court. One witness moved out of state and couldn't be found, the housekeeper wouldn't show up, and another who had identified Dr. Craig in a pivotal instance for the prosecution's case had changed their story in court.

To make matters even more suspicious, when the jury couldn't decide on whether or not there was a connection between Dr. Craig and Dr. Knabe's death, the judge stepped in as the thirteenth juror, ultimately ruling that Dr. Craig could not be charged with the murder of his alleged former fiancée. Alonzo benefited from this ruling as well, since he couldn't be a conspirator to a crime that legally didn't occur. Using his position as estate executor, many believe he bled her assets dry and pocketed her money. The documentation regarding her "insolvent estate" (by Alonzo's estimation) was rife with miscalculations and obvious errors. Personal items belonging to Dr. Knabe were never recovered, nor were the records of them ever being sold.

Dr. Knabe's body was ultimately buried in an unmarked grave at the Crown Hill Mausoleum in Indianapolis (something that was rectified some years after the horrors surrounding her demise came to light). Several newspapers have attempted to have her case reopened, but unfortunately, the original files and documents were destroyed in a 1977 flood.

The Living

- Craig Mince: As the new president of the Athenaeum Foundation, he needs to make sure it's safe for the local community members who frequent it on a daily basis. He also needs to reconcile with the reported activity while building upon the historical location's already illustrious reputation. If there is indeed paranormal activity occurring in the Athenaeum, we need to document it, understand it, and give Craig best practices on how to deal with it.

The Dead

- Do the supposed hauntings have to do with Dr. Helene Knabe? Either the doctor herself or the men who reportedly murdered her?

- There could any number of local visitors to the Athenaeum who could be lingering there; the building was a place of comfort for so many.

Investigation

When compiling research and potential points of interest that could serve our investigation, there was one story that stood out above all else: the sordid circumstances surrounding the death of Dr. Knabe.

Murder mysteries tend to be catnip for some paranormal investigators. There's an assumption, undoubtedly influenced by many classic horror films and ghost stories, that because someone was killed or died in a location, their spirit will persist there. With that knowledge in hand, some investigators will go full bore and base their entire case around the murder, oftentimes not researching all the facts associated with the individual they're now convinced is haunting said location.

When it comes to addressing any entities that may be in a location or establishing some sort of communication, it's always best to never assume who or what is present, which was the case with the Athenaeum. The building had served so many different people for so many years, so to put all of our investigative eggs in one basket and potentially exclude or alienate any entities there would be malpractice on our part. As always, we have clients with actual concerns and fears, and if we couldn't get the center's director answers, we'd not only be letting him down, but the thousands of people the Athenaeum serves as well.

Admittedly though, the more we learned about Dr. Knabe's life, her connection to the Athenaeum, her murder, and what transpired in her community afterward, the more difficult it was to ignore the possibility that she was behind the building's paranormal activity, or at least part of it.

Grandma's Attic

It was difficult for us to get excited for the possibility of experiencing anything paranormal in Grandma's Attic. While we go to great lengths to debunk any and every claim we're presented with, we are genuinely ecstatic to find proof of paranormal activity and phenomenon and subject it to scientific scrutiny.

This attic didn't give us any hope of doing that.

It seemed like we certainly got the short end of the stick when it came to initial investigative locations. There was a gorgeous,

haunted theater right beneath us that was begging to be investigated, along with an exercise room with claims of an ethereal
being floating out of a window. Then there was the dance hall right
beside the restaurant where reports of voices, laughter, and movement could be heard, even when no one was present.

The attic's claims, in short, sucked in comparison if you were
hoping to find any ghosts, at least in theory. When we were assigned
to it at the top of the first night of our investigation, it was difficult
to not feel like we were getting the shaft. The space lacked any concrete claims save for the mention of negative feelings and a sense
of dread and discomfort. As longtime investigators, this reeked to
us of easily debunkable phenomenon (i.e., folks getting the heebie-
jeebies due to easily explained environmental factors).

We'll pose this question: what old attic have you been in that
hasn't felt creepy?

Infrasound

Our primary goal going into Grandma's Attic, like every case,
was to get to the bottom of the claims. As far as this specific location
of the Athenaeum was concerned... there weren't really any. We
planned to get to the bottom of these negative feelings by sweeping
for electromagnetic frequency ranges (EMF) and using an OmniMic
that detects sounds for all locations, paired with a computer application that could detect ultralow frequencies (infrasound.)

Here's why this was an important part of our investigation:
prolonged exposure to EMF, even lower levels depending on
your brain's sensitivity, can cause a litany of different sensations,
thoughts, and feelings. It's been known to inflict headaches, nau-
sea, and sleeplessness, but could also instill ominous thoughts and,
in some rare cases, even depression and suicidal ruminations.

As for infrasound, these are noise frequencies that our inner ear picks up and registers in our brain, even if we don't audibly hear them. What we were looking for was a specific decibel range (85 or above) for sustained periods of time that were below 20 Hz. Being subjected to high levels of infrasound, over time, can have similar effects to EMF exposure. Extreme sensations of discomfort are what primarily result from high infrasound contamination, so much so that some filmmakers even mix the audio in their movies during key moments to upset viewers. The film *Irréversible*, for example, contains a horrifying assault scene that forced audience members to leave theaters, revolted at the uneasy and prolonged display. However, prior to that shocking moment, several people made their exit when the imagery on the screen wasn't as grotesque, deciding they had enough. Why? Because Director Gaspar Noé placed a specific ultralow frequency, 27 Hz [28] (just above infrasound), throughout the film's entire audio track, disquieting most viewers on a subconscious level without them even realizing it. Tons of other films use this same tactic to unsettle audiences, like *Paranormal Activity*, which would be a more appropriate reference, given the nature of our work.

> **Mustafa:** When we were first tasked with investigating Grandma's Attic, Brandon and I were honestly not thrilled. It was hard to feel like we weren't getting a bit fucked over when directly beneath us was an amazing theater that during the tour had all of the vibes of a legitimately spooky place. My hair stood up on the back

28. Natalie Zarrelli, "How the Hidden Sounds of Horror Movie Soundtracks Freak You Out," Atlas Obscura, October 31, 2016, https://www.atlasobscura.com/articles/how-the-hidden-sounds-of-horror-movie-soundtracks-freak-you-out.

of my neck when I first entered it and I felt like there was always someone walking around the hallways. Not necessarily lurking, but just waiting around, watching, curious. Even more of a tease was the fact that we helped set up cameras in the theater/auditorium. The restaurant area with the dance floor also seemed like a better option than the attic. We planned to keep our run rather short—go in, find a natural explanation for why people were feeling the way they were feeling, and get out.

We made our way to Grandma's Attic with our Data Logger (which detects a variety of different environmental conditions, including EMF) and OmniMic, ready to debunk this uncomfortable feeling.

Getting to the tiny room wasn't an easy task; we walked through the theater and back up behind the stage, gazing longingly at the space we ACTUALLY wanted to investigate (in due time, we would), through a tiny door you wouldn't realize was there unless someone told you. Parts of the stairwell weren't air-conditioned, and we were investigating this location smack dab in the middle of July during one of the hottest weeks of Indiana's summer. To call it oppressively stifling would be an understatement.

When we walked farther up the stairs, the smell of stone and old wood helped to round out the sauna-esque vibe we experienced through our labyrinthine trek to Grandma's Attic. At the uppermost point of the building stood the room. We looked around and immediately noticed bird droppings on the floor and walls of the hallway, which were a wonderful accompaniment to our sweat and hundred-year lignum musk.

Opening the door to Grandma's Attic immediately revealed what we believed was the first cause of the negative feelings people experience there: the funhouse effect.

Since it was located on the uppermost point of the building, this particular space, like many attics or bonus rooms in a building, wasn't designed for aesthetics. The ceiling was taller in some areas than others. The exposed brick jutted out more in particular sections, and the extremely long and narrow room, coupled with the obscene heat, would make anyone who languished there for more than two minutes pretty desperate. Or maybe even get to thinking something weird was afoot.

After noting the room's unconventional construction, we conducted an EMF sweep to determine if there were any pockets of the room with consistently above-average readings. Save for a few spots with some negligible aberrances where it's normal for EMF to be higher (directly near outlets, light fixtures, etc.), it was clear that electromagnetic frequencies were not causing the gnarly feelings those who spent time in the attic experienced.

Infrasound, however, was a completely different story. After setting up our OmniMic and monitoring the frequencies it picked up in the area, we were consistently hitting high levels of infrasound—it hovered around 80 dB and would occasionally shoot up over 90 dB. What makes this finding even more significant is when you consider the environmental conditions in which we were investigating: it was well into the night when both car and foot traffic from the outside were at a minimum. Additionally, the hum of various appliances that would be on in the Athenaeum during the day were mostly shut off. Plus, we were surrounded by a team of people who are trained to work as quietly as possible in order for us to carry out our experiments with little to no contamination. So if the infrasound, under those conditions, was that high, then it was safe to assume that during the day it would be even greater.

We were thoroughly convinced we'd sufficiently debunked the feelings of dread in Grandma's Attic. Upon seeing and feeling the funhouse effects, along with the high levels of infrasound that could adversely influence temporal lobe activity, it was a no-brainer, and we were sure there was nothing paranormal afoot there.

Here's where things get interesting. We left our Data Logger near the attic's entrance while we conducted our infrasound measurement session in case it detected any other environmental changes. We only noticed it did just as we were about to wrap up our run.

We heard a noise in the hallway as we were about to walk out, which was followed by temperature and pressure changes registering on the Data Logger. While temperature changes, especially increases, would make sense given how sweltering it was in that attic, that didn't account for the sudden shift in barometric pressure, which is indicated by a flashing, yellow light.

We were a bit stunned and at a loss for words for good reason: we both *thought we had heard someone in the hallway*, even though there was no one there and our Data Logger was registering abnormal changes in the environment. It was a hair-raising moment for sure.

We were on the brink of wrapping up, and now it felt like something truly special was occurring out of nowhere; our presumed open-and-shut-case of debunking the claims in the attic had morphed into a potential session with a possible intelligent entity that had learned to manipulate our technology for communicative purposes.

So, we immediately conducted a session, incredulous as to what was occurring. We had both researched the history of Dr. Knabe through local records, period news articles, and the research laid out in Nicole Kobrowski's book, including the doctor's tragic end. We didn't want to lead with this information, however, because when attempting to establish contact with an entity, it's unwise to automatically assume or jump the gun as to who is there and indulge false positives, a methodology our team rigorously adhered to.

Funnily enough, the heat and stank of the attic didn't bother us at all and as excited as we were, we stuck to investigative protocol. Here's what we knew: it seemed that for whatever reason, whoever was there was interested in our Data Logger and could influence environmental changes on it, or, in attempting to interact with us, caused sharp shifts in temperature and pressure.

We instructed the entity on how to interact with us using the Data Logger to provide yes or no questions. We needed to establish this as a baseline of communications.

"We believe you're trying to communicate with us, and we thank you for that. We'd like to ask you some questions. If you understand and would like to answer yes, could you interact with that grey box on the floor with orange numbers and set those lights off again, please?"

Another yellow flash. We waited, and repeated the question, apologizing for being repetitive but reaffirmed our desire to decidedly conclude we were indeed communicating with Dr. Knabe. After several confirmations with pressure changes, we started our line of questioning, casting a wide net. We asked the entity if they were a woman. Pressure light goes off. We asked if they were a man. Nothing happened. We asked if they're a woman again and the pressure light goes off.

It was at that moment we both knew who we were probably speaking to, but we had to be absolutely certain. We asked if they were a guest in the Athenaeum. No response. We asked if they were an employee: a positive response. We asked if they were a student here. No response. We asked if they were a teacher: a positive response. We asked if they taught health and science. Positive response. We asked if we were speaking with Dr. Knabe—positive response.

Holy moly.

We began to push and ask why she was here while throwing out possible reasons, asking her to confirm or deny them, but nothing further happened in our session. There weren't any more readings on the Data Logger, not even temperature. Even though our session went cold, so to speak, we were both stunned and eager to bring this data back to the team.

If you've ever been on a ghost-hunting event, you'll likely find a large number of people huddled in different corners of the room, printed sheets of paper in their hands as they rattle off names historically associated with the location, staring at various gadgets hoping for a response. This interaction was different.

What we experienced in Grandma's Attic was, by all accounts, a paranormal jackpot. The entity was apparently intuitive and curious and demonstrably grasped our line of questioning with ease by responding immediately. Using control questions, we were able to provide some fairly convincing evidence we just established contact with Dr. Knabe, and given her lauded scientific acumen, it made sense she would be intrigued with such a fascinating piece of equipment. We even theorized that she may have been attracted to and hopefully impressed by our methodology. (We'll keep telling ourselves that, real recognize real and such.)

The Concert

We rejoined the team on the first-floor lobby of the Athenaeum and shared our find, walking through the methodology of how we communicated with Dr. Knabe. The other team members spoke about their individual runs: they'd hear noises, knocks, and movement whenever they'd bring up facets of the Athenaeum's history. Theater shows, musical events, social dances, which seemed to confirm what we had gathered in Grandma's Attic: that there are intelligent entities present in the Athenaeum, and they have a strong emotional connection to the building and what took place there. That's when we learned there was a plan for enticing any entities in the building into the theater: by staging a four-string quartet performance of music from the period.

We were immediately excited by this idea, as the human element cannot be ignored in any field of scientific study, especially when it comes to the paranormal. Theoretically, entities are tied to a specific location due to an intense bond they share with it. If we were entities, we'd much rather spend our time being entertained and enjoying ourselves by indulging in the things we love, not flit about being miserable all of the time, reliving the worst day of our existence.

We decided to make the experience as true to the day as possible; we weren't simply going to blare the music from loudspeakers, but instead arrange for a live band to perform the pieces. Dr. Knabe, during her heyday, enjoyed the live plays and concerts that took place at the Athenaeum along with her friends, family, and coworkers. We hoped that by replicating an experience she had there while she was alive that Dr. Knabe, or any other entities that were there, would be compelled to come to the theater and watch.

We needed to prepare the theater for the investigation and wanted to cover the area with as many pieces of tech as possible that could document the presence of any entities. We scattered Data Loggers across multiple tables along with recorders, with one on the stage, which we'd review after the fact, in case we caught voices or the reported chatter/dancing that visitors claimed to hear in the area. We walked to the back of the theater and up the stairwell that led to the soundboard. It stood high above the entire theater and we placed a 4K lockoff camera there that provided a master shot of the entire theater, just in case one of the reported shadow figures ambled in to catch a glimpse of the show.

This was easily one of the biggest orchestrated efforts we'd put together to date in an investigation and every member of the team was present to monitor any environmental conditions that would register on our equipment. The air was electric, and you could tell every member of the team and crew was waiting with bated breath as the performers took the stage, wondering if this was going to work. A single, pale ghost light lit up the stage, a theater tradition we decided to partake in that was all too appropriate for our case. As *Playbill* puts it: "A ghost light is a single bulb left burning whenever a theatre is dark. Some argue that its function is to chase away mischievous spirits; others insist it lights the way for the ghosts that are said to inhabit virtually every theatre, keeping them happy and contented."[29] Under that amber glow from the single, stationary light, our equipment situated, our senses sharpened, we were ready to investigate when that first chord was struck, and music filled the theater.

---

29. Lindsey Wilson, "Why Do Broadway Theatres Keep a 'Ghost Light' Burning on the Stage?" Playbill, September 19, 2008, https://www.playbill.com /article/ask-playbillcom-the-ghost-light-com-153440.

> **Mustafa:** I had so much fun watching this performance
> and just soaking up the moment that I almost forgot I
> was there to investigate. When I looked slightly to my
> left, I thought I saw something and so I gave chase with
> another member of the team. However, it was gone.
> We couldn't catch it or document any of its movements
> on camera. Such a shame, because I really enjoyed their
> playing. If there was an entity up there, I wish it had
> come down to the table area with us instead of chilling
> on the balcony.

The band's playing had definitely drummed up activity. It didn't take long for pressure changes to register on several Data Loggers as the band played. We darted our eyes from the equipment to the hallways under the swell of the band's playing; Athenaeum employees reportedly saw shadows walking through the hallways and we wanted to see if our trap cameras were triggered by any movement. In the throes of one piece, one team member darted toward the hallway, believing he saw a shadow figure on the left-hand balcony, something another member of our team saw as well. While this occurred, our Data Loggers continued to register punctuated changes in barometric pressure.

We attempted to follow the shadow figure throughout the hallway and into side rooms, but we were led back into the theater, our breathless camera crew following quickly behind us while reviewing their footage, hoping to catch a glimpse of what other team members had seen, but there was nothing on the recordings we could see at that time.

When the band stopped playing, the charged energy in the theater was palpable and, notably, the pressure changes on our Data Loggers stopped. This was the second instance where we witnessed what appeared to be a presence when we actively attempted to reach out, whether it be through conversation or song.

We took a few minutes to discuss the real-time environmental changes we witnessed and gave a play-by-play of the sequence of events that led to the mad dash for the shadow figure. Another team member suggested that we (Brandon and Mustafa) stay behind in the theater and attempt to establish contact with an entity as we had some compelling interactions in Grandma's Attic, especially because of the intriguing pressure aberrations that occurred while the band played.

The rest of the team and the majority of the camera crew exited the theater. We were left with a single camera operator, an audio recorder, and two Data Loggers. The ghost light still burning on stage, we set up a logger on a ledge situated on the right-hand side of the theater. At first we waited and looked around, hoping to catch another glimpse of the shadow figure, and maybe make sense of what we experienced.

Eventually we introduced ourselves again and referenced the attic, asking if there was anyone present with us. A yellow light blinked on our Data Logger, once, twice. We followed up by asking if we were speaking to a woman: another blink on our Data Logger. We waited and made sure it wasn't some other environmental condition setting off the Data Logger. Nothing. We asked yet again if we were speaking to a woman, and the yellow light flashed again. Then we asked if we had the pleasure of speaking with Dr. Knabe and we were met with another flash of light. We continued our line of questioning and the session turned into what was one of our longest sustained interaction sessions we've ever had. Dr. Knabe (presumably) reached out to us over and over again.

What we believe to be a paranormal entity had become very chatty when we brought up the performance. We asked several times if they enjoyed it, and pressure changes would occur every single time. When we thanked who we believed to be Dr. Knabe for being with us several times, we were met with pressure changes. When we stopped asking questions, the Data Logger was quiet. Again, when we asked control questions like if we were speaking to a man, a librarian, a child, someone who works in the gymnasium, we'd get nothing. To experience that kind of live communication and to consistently document it in the moment was truly remarkable.

When we decided to transition the topic of conversation to intimations about Dr. Knabe's death, activity on the Data Logger halted. We elected not to push the conversation in that direction because when we tried, we were met with silence on the Data Logger. So we shifted our line of questioning back to the performance and whether or not whoever was there enjoyed it, and we started seeing pressure changes register on the device again. It was clear there were certain avenues of discussion that would not yield responses, and others that would.

Another reason we decided not to push our talk toward the doctor's murder is that, theoretically, some entities might not understand that they have passed away or are dead. The truth is we don't know what the afterlife looks like. Empirically speaking it's impossible to surmise that the type of afterlife we've been conditioned by cultural, literary, and religious traditions actually exists. These entities that we're possibly communicating with could be living out their lives in stasis (i.e., in a point in time where they were alive, thriving, and going about their daily routines). Or we could be speaking to them in a sliver of time. In the case of Dr. Knabe, it could have been a day or night she was enjoying in the Athenaeum and for all intents and purposes, she could believe that she was very much alive.

Whatever that plane of existence was for Dr. Knabe, it appeared the character of her individual personality somehow remained intact. Her specific curiosities persisted, as did her peculiar wants and predilections. A fondness for music of her era, filled with love for her work, and an unkillable desire to take delight in a place that warmed her heart while she was alive.

For the two of us to not only be a part of that, but capture it, was a privilege we'll never forget.

Our Conclusion

Brandon: By conducting the experiment in the theater, it set the perfect stage for Mustafa and me to continue our earlier line of questioning with who we believed to be Dr. Knabe. Seeing the difference in the change of the environment made it that much more exciting for us. The pressure changes we recorded in response to our questions was a breakthrough moment for the classification system and furthering the science of the field. Sitting back and looking over all of our analyses and data, I concluded that the Athenaeum falls under a Class One: Grey Lady. The tragic history of Dr. Knabe and the direct communication and environmental data have led us to believe that Dr. Knabe was indeed murdered for the sake of love and that she is trying to relay her story in death.

— 6 —

PARANORMAL MALPRACTICE

Throughout the United States there are many historical buildings that have purported ghostly activity. Many of these sites are run by historical societies, state governments, and museums. Yet, there are a select few that are privately owned and operated. Para-tourism can be a very lucrative business for many of these locations. When running a site that allows para-tourism, the owners of these build ings have an obligation to maintain the historical integrity of these sites. As soon as there is no accountability with historical facts and integrity when it comes to investigating the site, it becomes what we refer to as paranormal malpractice. Upon arriving at Madison Seminary, we started to notice a strange trend.

If you're a paranormal enthusiast on the prowl for haunts in the Ohio area, chances are you've visited, or at least heard of, the Madison Seminary. But despite its popularity, no matter where we conducted historical research, each account of Madison Seminary's history seemed to vary by the source. We learned very quickly that there was a lot of controversy surrounding the building and its history.

Years of paranormal investigation and para-tourism seems to have blurred the lines separating fact from fiction at Madison Seminary. During the walk-through, a clear pattern of negative events in the former facility emerged. According to the eyewitnesses, almost every square foot of the seminary had some kind of negative activity manifesting. One major question had to be asked: When did the rise in negative events start to take place? After walking through the building and hearing the many years of reported activity, Mustafa was left with the monumental task to find facts supporting the claims of abuse in the facility.

Self-Manifested (Pseudo) Haunting at Madison Seminary

- Madison, Ohio. Investigated in 2019 on A&E's *Ghost Hunters*. (Season one, episode six, "There's Something in the Seminary.")

Claims

- Spirits remain of traumatized female patients sexually assaulted by doctors.
- Sudden feelings of illness, stomach pains.
- Visitors report being touched, even strangled.
- Feeling of being watched.
- Motion detectors triggered in empty rooms.
- Disembodied voices.
- Footsteps heard in empty hallways.
- Intelligent knocking in response to questions.

History

While the Madison Seminary today is vaunted for its ghostly occurrences and rumors embodying a sordid history that would make Hollywood horror screenwriters salivate, the seminary started as just what its name implies: a college and learning institution that was heavily steeped in religious studies.[30]

The expansive campus stemmed from a humble initial structure that was first chartered in 1845, located a little over three miles away from the coast of Lake Erie. It took two years to complete the building, which soon became inhabited with students in the pursuit of a better education than what was immediately afforded to them in the area. The seminary became so popular over its first dozen years that another structure was built on its campus grounds: 1859 saw the first dorms on the premises. In its busiest and most bustling of years, some 150 students lived, learned, and thrived at this location.

However, the establishment of Madison Seminary came right before the Morrill Act of 1862,[31] the first major instance in the USA where federal aid was distributed on a grand scale to education. The act paved the groundwork for a larger connected network and a national push for public schools. Government-owned lands were reserved for the establishment of educational institutions, which inevitably and slowly decreased the need for private ones. This was bad news for Madison Seminary's future as a bustling academy.

In 1890, a second Morrill Act was introduced that broadened the reach of granted lands for schools all across the country, so by the

---

30. "The Madison Home: From a Grand Army to Ghosts," Ohio Memory, April 13, 2018, https://ohiomemory.ohiohistory.org/archives/3768.

31. "Morrill Act," Ourdocuments.gov, https://www.ourdocuments.gov/doc .php?flash=false&doc=33.

end of the century public education was gaining traction on a federal level. This resulted in an even steeper decline of student enrollment in private facilities. Madison Seminary's student attendance numbers consequently suffered. The seminary's days as a private institution were numbered.

The building received a golden parachute of sorts, however, and it found a new purpose thanks to national concern about the treatment of Civil War survivors. President and former Union colonel Benjamin Harrison vowed to dole out pensions to veterans as part of his 1888 election campaign, a promise which was not only kept, but extended to soldiers and veterans who were disabled, which included out-of-service citizens as well. The Ohio Women's Relief Corps saw this as an opportunity to care for Ohio families who were affected by the Civil War. They received money from Harrison's pension initiative to acquire the Madison Seminary campus.

The school buildings were then renovated and transformed into homes for Civil War nurses as well as women who were displaced by the war. Widows, sisters, and mothers of soldiers all had access to boarding and care thanks to the efforts of the Women's Relief Corps (W.R.C.) and Grand Army of the Republic (G.A.R.)., who also commissioned a new wing of the building. The Madison Seminary officially became the Madison Home. It was bigger than ever and returned to being a bustling structure teeming with residents benefiting from the services it provided. Once it offered education; now it offered relief for so many Ohio residents who were in dire need of a helping hand.

Civil War Spies

While many of the Madison Home's new residents never saw Civil War combat, a look into the location's records is filled with some fascinating finds, like the fact that Elizabeth Stiles once lived there. Elizabeth was a politically vocal seamstress and teacher who often decried the Confederacy and made her pro-Union stance very known. Unsurprisingly, this fomented a fair share of controversy in Kansas, a state politically divided over the Civil War. This controversy would culminate in a familial tragedy that would forever change the course of Elizabeth's life.

She had moved to Kansas with her husband, Jacob Stiles, whom she met and lived with in Chicago. While she could, for the most part, openly discuss her political views in Illinois, her outspokenness in Kansas did not go unnoticed. Quantrill's Raiders, a group of Confederate bushwhackers, weren't fond of Elizabeth's political views and one night went to her and Jacob's home. Jacob was murdered. A widowed mother fueled by revenge, Elizabeth doubled down on her hatred of the Confederacy and jumped at the opportunity directly offered to her by Abraham Lincoln to go behind enemy lines to gain vital intel as a spy for Union forces.

She would often pose as an antebellum grandmother searching for her granddaughter (who was actually her own thirteen-year-old daughter, Clara). Other times, she'd work as a Confederate nurse and listen in on the conversations of soldiers and high-ranking military officers and then relay the information back to her Northern contacts. She was once apprehended in Jefferson City, Missouri, and interrogated by Confederate authorities, but was so adept at persuasion she successfully convinced an officer she was actually a spy for the South. Not only did the arresting officer let her go free, but he also gave Elizabeth a horse and a firearm upgrade to carry out her clandestine operations.

In 1864 Elizabeth's cover was officially blown, forcing her to retire from the world of Civil War espionage. Her son cared for her until 1895, when she was placed in the Madison Home for elder care. She passed away in the home approximately three years later in 1898. There was yet another female Union spy, Mary E. Truesdale, who lived in the Madison Home as well. She passed away in 1906, but not much is known about her life.

Truesdale died two years after the Women's Relief Corps could no longer bear the financial burden to own and operate the facility, prompting the organization to relegate ownership to the state of Ohio in 1904. While the Madison Home had changed hands and management, it still functioned as a bastion of support and hope for local veterans and their families for decades.

In 1962, ownership of the building was then given to the state's Department of Mental Hygiene and Corrections, which resulted in war widows returning home to live with their respective families or moving into other nursing facilities in Ohio. It's during this time the most recent paranormal lore surrounding Madison Seminary started to materialize.

A Second Chance

The following thirteen or so years the building housed psychiatric patients, intellectually disabled women, and female inmates from Cleveland State Hospital and the Ohio Reformatory for Women, with recommendations from the Madison Township administrative board. Until 1975, the Madison Home operated under the name Opportunity Village (O.V.),[32] which primarily

---

32. Debbie Palinsky, "History of the Ohio Cottage building," *Star Beacon*, October 31, 2009, https://www.starbeacon.com/archives/history-of-the-ohio-cottage-building/article_164fcb1d-287b-5959-ba0c-1123a67eb73f.html.

housed and helped care for intellectually disabled individuals who were mostly self-sufficient, but required a bit of assistance. O.V. was also a home to inmates with a history of good behavior and favorable recommendations from the Ohio Reformatory for Women in Marysville. The Ohio Bureau of Vocational Rehabilitation worked closely with O.V. to develop programs and implement services that would assist both intellectually disabled residents and inmates in acquiring job training and a variety of vocational skills so they could better integrate into society and hold gainful employment.

In 1975, Opportunity Village closed after funding for its provided programs was pulled, and over several decades the building exchanged hands through various sellers and primarily remained empty, undergoing several renovations in the process. This went on until May 21, 1998, when the Lake County Board of Commissioners sold the building and its property at public auction for $28,500 to John Cassell, owner of Cass-Mill Nurseries. It was primarily used for storage and office space, but an agreement was made with the Madison Historical Society that designated a portion of the building's square footage to highlight the area's cultural history by showcasing an assortment of period pieces, artifacts, and news clippings of significant events.

The building's current owner investigated the building in 2013 while filming a paranormal web series and purchased it in 2016. He and his team of paranormal investigators have uploaded several videos pertaining to the location's ghostly history and strange claims, which was the impetus for our interest and own casework at Madison Seminary.

The Living

• The building's owner is convinced the building has a dark past given the experiences he and visitors to Madison Seminary have had. Can we document any of the paranormal activity there?

The Dead

• Can the activity be attributed to some of the notable figures associated with the property like Elizabeth Stiles?

• Were there female patients and inmates who were abused and assaulted by an evil doctor?

• Are there any inimical entities present who pose a threat to those who visit the seminary?

Investigation

Brandon: Following Mustafa's extensive historical research, he was able to uncover a tremendous amount of documentation through the local historical society. A clear picture was painted that the legends about abuse that surround Madison Seminary seemed to be just that, legends. Mustafa and I wanted to walk through the building before the investigation to see if we could find any physical signs of mistreatment or trauma. According to the eyewitnesses and owner of the building, there are many stories of sexual abuse, physical torture, and murder. Since the historical records showed no signs of any mistreatment, we had to be thorough and look for physical signs ourselves.

Mustafa: Arriving on a hot summer day in the Madison Seminary was, as strange as it may sound, a beautiful experience. After hearing about the claims of abused women at the hands of deranged doctors, of a rumored murder that occurred in the basement, and tales of visitors being choked or women having their hair played with, an image of the location was created in my mind. I'm sure it was the same for my fellow team members. I half expected to roll up to Madison and see a haunted mansion with storm clouds and lightning cracking in the background. However, I was greeted with a large, gorgeous campus with trees and flowers swaying in the wind before it. I couldn't wait to get inside and get to work to see if we could document, re-create, experience, or debunk any of the paranormal claims that were reported by the building's owner.

While the Madison Seminary looked stately and inviting on its exterior, the inside of the building belied its outdoor beauty. It didn't help that it operated as a haunted house on some days during the year and was decorated with deranged-looking dolls and other spooky tropes. But there was another decorative trend we noticed throughout our initial tour of the building and that was the recurring imagery of specific sigils painted on nearly every floor of the main building. We found them scrawled on windows, the glass panels of doors, and on dangling pieces of wallpaper, semi-hidden in some areas. After finding more and more of these symbols, we began to notice that there was a correlating directional pattern. We found sigils on the east, west, north, and south portions on nearly every floor on the main building.

I Need This to Work

We snapped several photos of the sigils. We wanted to know what they could possibly mean, so we started with a broad search of ancient symbols and rune markings but didn't find anything that correlated with what was scrawled on the seminary's walls. That's when we learned of the building owner's initial interview with other members of the team. A specific comment that he made perked up our ears. He said, "I need this to work" after talking about all the money he had personally invested in the seminary.

That, coupled with our own initial conversations, gave us the impression he was not only *adamant* about Madison Seminary being haunted, but the hauntings stemmed from past trauma and patient abuse, much of it sexual in nature. He also informed us that shortly after acquiring the building, he found documentation indicating large orders of antipsychotics and other medication that were delivered to the building, but couldn't locate it at that moment.

When we delved back into our research of the sigils, we did so with the impression that the owner was convinced of a dark narrative surrounding the seminary's past, despite the fact that we initially couldn't locate any recorded evidence that this was the case. That's when we decided to look at occultist symbolism and imagery. It wasn't long before we noticed there were strong similarities between the sigils that were recently drawn on multiple floors of the seminary's main building and summoning spells from *Goetia: The Lesser Key of Solomon*,[33] which is also referred to as the real-life Necronomicon,[34] aka, *The Book of the Dead*.

---

33. Aleister Crowley and S.L. MacGregor Mathers, *The Lesser Key of Solomon*, 1904.

34. H.P. Lovecraft, *The History of the Necronomicon*, 1938.

We sent photos of the sigils, without any context, to colleagues who study occultist imagery. They said the drawings looked like attempted recreations of these symbols, and then asked about the location of the sigils on the walls. Again, this was without any provided context on our part. When we informed our colleagues that there was a recurring compass theme of east, west, north, south on each floor of the main building, their response wasn't a positive one. They told us that whoever was there was attempting to conjure and/or trap an entity in the area and that we should be careful.

However, the client comes first, and Madison Seminary's owner was not only gracious enough to allow us to investigate the storied location but appeared to be very ardent in assisting us in any capacity with our work. Additionally, he was working on providing us with documentation to support his claims about the building's dark past, so we didn't want to jump to any conclusions about his intentions.

Above all, however, was the fact that save for Daryl, no other member of the team had investigated Madison Seminary before, and you really can't get a feel for a place until you've delved into it yourself. And we were excited to experience the location for ourselves.

Civil War Building

Once night fell, and the July heat somewhat subsided, we tackled the Civil War building first, keeping in mind everything we learned regarding the building's history and our interactions with its owner. This was the same building famous women like Elizabeth Stiles and Mary E. Truesdale had lived in, along with so many other countless individuals the seminary helped to educate, care for, rehabilitate, and house since its inception in the mid-1800s. Although it was evident that parts of the building were in disrepair, with many of its original edifications still intact, it was apparent that the seminary was originally constructed to be a stalwart structure meant to stand the test of time.

One of the first runs we conducted was in a long, narrow hallway punctuated by rooms once inhabited by the building's many residents. The eerie quiet amplified our footsteps through the halls as we canvassed the area with our FLIR thermal imaging camera. If there were reported footsteps heard in the hallway, could we corroborate an image to accompany those sounds? As always, we set up our ambisonic microphone to document any Electronic Voice Phenomena we could listen for during evidence review and an EDI+ Data Logger to monitor any changes in environmental conditions. We also compiled a historical list of resident and employee names who had either lived and/or worked at the Madison Seminary. This served a dual purpose: would reading off the names trigger any activity in the course of our investigation? Or, if our audio recorder did manage to pick up a name in our attempts to establish contact with a possible entity, would that name appear on our list? We settled ourselves in the hallway and began to call out the names on the list.

Rattling them off didn't seem to initially entice any entities or spur any activity. We stood there in the dark, saying a name, calling out to any of the past residents of the home and waiting for one, two, three, four, five seconds between each name with bated breath and our eyes darting back and forth between the FLIR thermal camera and the Data Logger. Would an environmental change indicate we spurred some activity? Would we hear a footstep or knocking noise like so many other investigators reported? But the only response to the dozens of names we called out was silence. Or so we thought. There wasn't a significant amount of activity occurring on our Data Logger, save for a pressure change. Nothing that seemed to suggest there was anything present that was attempting to directly communicate with us through our devices.

That is, until we heard what sounded like a woman's voice calling out in the distance, washed away, trying to break through to us in the night air. Which name were they reacting to? Or was it even a woman's voice? We read back the names, listening even more intently, our eyes widened, ears strained, anticipating a follow-up response. But there was nothing, at least in the moment, and we exited the hallway with our equipment in tow to explore other parts of the seminary.

On Our Way to the Basement

We explored the Civil War building as quietly as we could, taking in the history and keeping our eyes and ears open for any movement our presence may stir up. With each step through the halls as we peered into more and more rooms, we both agreed the feeling in this area was different from the hallway we had just investigated. The still air was permeated with a tension we couldn't exactly place, and we experienced firsthand the claim reported by other investigators: we certainly felt like we were being watched. Then the quiet was suddenly disrupted by the sound of movement from one of the rooms. We ran toward the area it emitted from: an empty classroom. Could it be linked to the voice we thought we heard? There was only a short window to document any potential strange activity, so we immediately set our Data Logger on a desk in the classroom and conducted a session to see if there would be any environmental changes. While one of us asked questions about the building's history and brought up pertinent facts about its residents, the other set up motion detectors as a corroborating device.

Again, we spoke about the building's Civil War history, and mentioned some names of its residents. No changes registered on our equipment. That's when we decided to reference some of the alleged violent claims. The room was filled with a glowing yellow light emanating from the Data Logger, a signal that sudden changes in barometric pressure occurred. We waited to see if the device would register a change again before we repeated the question to see if we could replicate what just occurred, but then the room filled with a pale, blue light, cracking the darkness. It was the motion detector.

We stared at the device, waiting to see if its blue light would die down. There was nothing in front of it and none of us had moved passed it, but something had set it off. As the light began to fade, we asked if whoever was there could confirm their presence.

That's when simultaneous pressure and temperature changes began to register on the Data Logger, immediately followed by our motion detector's light triggering on, then fading, then turning back on again repeatedly.

We attempted to further the conversation and instructed whatever was setting off our devices to do so again, intentionally, as if to answer "yes" to our questions. And while we had several instances where this occurred, the activity seemed to die down. If something or someone was interacting with our devices, it became clear they were no longer engaging with us, so we decided to further canvass the area and proceeded to venture into the building's basement.

We had no idea what was in store for us. And looking back at the investigation now, something leads me to believe we had cornered someone or something that didn't want to be bothered.

The Basement

We made our way through the main building and down the concrete steps leading to the basement. While the July heat didn't permeate this area, making it naturally colder than other parts of the building, there was one room in particular that immediately gave us chills. We were both silently drawn to the first room on the right and wandered in without saying a word to one another. We set up motion detectors in the recessed stone windowsills of the basement and strategically angled them so we could see their blue lights shine through the cold darkness.

We waited and listened. The feeling of being watched that we experienced upstairs felt considerably amplified, but we didn't know if it was a funhouse effect of being encased in grey concrete. So we reached out and asked if there was anyone present.

Almost instantly our motion detectors went off and we began registering pressure and temperature changes on the Data Logger. It was the classroom on steroids; however, just like the classroom, the activity spiked and then stopped. We persisted, asking more questions, and while the activity halted on our devices, we began hearing noises in other parts of the basement.

It appeared that whatever we had happened upon wasn't open to communicating with us. In this moment, we earned our *Ghost Hunters* moniker as we chased down whatever was causing our devices to register these environmental changes. We heard noises from outside of the room and we followed it down a narrow corridor. Through the shuffling of our feet on the dusty floor, other noises could be heard in yet another room. It felt disrespectful to chase down an entity that was attempting to distance itself from us, but the activity we were documenting was truly bizarre and we wanted to get to the bottom of it.

The sounds we heard shifted into another room, yet again, one that appeared to be a classroom with a chalkboard and desks. Prior to stepping inside, we had an ominous feeling that we should not enter, but we persisted. Nothing was inside the room. Were our minds playing tricks on us? Did we succumb to a shared paranoid episode where we fed our own delusions? It's possible, but that didn't account for our devices that were constantly being set off by invisible occurrences we couldn't readily explain.

As we walked out of the classroom, the motion detectors in the empty room by the basement stairs were set off, further suggesting that there was something attempting to escape our presence. We headed inside where the blue lights of not one but two of our motion detectors were pulsing, along with temperature and pressure changes registering on our Data Logger.

We tried wrapping our head around the activity while apologizing for agitating whoever was present. There was a mounting, palpable tension, coupled with our chase of the entity, and the constant triggering of multiple devices.

All of it culminated in a loud *crack* that struck the floor. When the sound erupted in the room, there wasn't a single pair of feet on the ground.

A rock was tossed right at our team. Out of nowhere.

Brandon: After the rock was thrown, I immediately asked Mustafa to hand me the Data Logger to see if we could document any environmental changes associated with the event. As soon as I walked in the direction where the rock was thrown, we had rapid pressure and temperature changes registering on the Data Logger. Not long after that I felt the sensation of a cold breeze pass through me. Right after the sensation stopped, I started to feel sick as if I was going to vomit. This was the first time I ever encountered a sensation of something passing through me. We were lucky enough to have multiple pieces of data to back up these experiences.

Mustafa: Anyone who's ever investigated the paranormal with a production team knows that the roles of camera men, producers, and sound engineers has them solely focused on their respective jobs, as Brandon and I were in ours. When we exited the room to go into the hallway, however, I saw Brandon keel over, suddenly not feeling well. He said he felt something cold pass through his body and that his stomach hurt immensely. When that happened, I could see that our production crew was less concerned about their sound levels and how well the moment was captured on their cameras, and more about the spooky activity and strange vibe that had just settled into the basement.

Brandon, ever the professional, immediately called for me to hand him the Data Logger after the rock was thrown and a wave of cold air went through his body. I did, and sure enough we registered pressure and temperature changes on the device.

Where did the rock come from? We checked the ceiling: no signs of any cracks or loose bits of concrete. We immediately located a sizable, jagged stone on the floor, and heard noises from other parts of the basement. We gave chase, yet again, and felt the same strange sensation as we did in the first room, mainly a feeling of heaviness in the air. Each step we took was filled with suspense and there was a collective holding of breath, as if at any moment a jump scare was waiting, or a metaphorical guillotine was hanging above our heads and we had no idea when the blade would drop.

That made it especially eerie walking into this area, almost as if we cornered something that wanted us gone. Again, there was no activity being registered on the Data Logger until we reached the very end of the room when we documented pressure and temperature changes, followed by nothing. This was then followed by more noises in the hallway and back to the room closest to where the rock was thrown. It's as if we surprised whoever or whatever was there, it/they would flee, and then we'd chase it down and the cycle repeated itself.

That's when our sound engineer began calling to us, alerting everyone to the fact that the motion detector had gone off. While no one was in the room. After several attempts to communicate with the entity and feeling as if we were encroaching on someone's personal space, making whoever it was uncomfortable, and adding Brandon's sudden sickness to the mix, we decided to exit the basement out of respect for any entity or entities that were there. It was time to review the audio and video footage, including plenty of careful looks at the rock-throwing incident.

While reviewing footage of our time in the basement, we couldn't provide any explanation for the rock being lobbed in Brandon's direction the way it was. If anything, the video footage solidified that it was indeed thrown by someone or something. Every member of our team was present on camera; no human being in that area tossed the stone. So where did it come from? It's a question that baffles us to this day.

Interestingly enough, Brandon wasn't the only member of our crew to feel ill during the case. A cameraman had fallen inexplicably ill earlier in the day, seemingly out of nowhere. So much so that he was unavailable for filming and needed to return to the hotel to sleep. Another member of our team claimed they felt ill during their run as well; they experienced similar stomach pains several moments before Brandon's cold spell episode. It's interesting to note that these team members were investigating the attic area at the same time we explored the basement.

Evidence Review

The most significant piece of visual evidence captured at the Madison Seminary didn't actually occur in the basement where we experienced most of the real-time activity, but rather in the hallway of the Civil War building. While conducting our investigation and attempting to establish a connection to any present entities, we discovered a phenomenon on the FLIR thermal imaging camera that defies practical explanation.

Toward the end of the hallway, through the window of a door that led to a fire escape, we captured what appears to be the head of an individual walking past it with the same heat signature as its surroundings. What's so breathtaking about this find is that whatever was walking on the fire escape was walking to ... nothing.

Structurally speaking, there's just a railing located where the individual walked, and we were on the second floor of the building when it was captured. We confirmed that no one was on the fire escape at the time (a difficult spot to reach) nor did anyone climb it during our entire time filming at the Madison Seminary. The figure moved slowly as well and judging from the evidence, was relatively short, no taller than five feet and three inches.

We also captured an EVP of what sounds like a disembodied woman's voice. But what could it mean? Did this have anything to do with the claims of Madison Seminary's alleged history of abused patients? We decided to see if there was any validity to the more unsavory claims regarding the building's past.

Mustafa: After digging deep into Madison Seminary's history and meeting with the director of the Madison Historical Society, I couldn't find any evidence to support that physical and sexual abuse had taken place on the premises as our client suggested. Not during the days when it was a Civil War veterans' home, not during its time as a haven for veterans' families, not when it was operated by the department of mental hygiene, nor when it was Opportunity Village and housed inmates. There were no newspaper articles and the society's director, who is a lifelong resident of Madison, had never heard anything negative about the building. There were also no historical records that a doctor had murdered a nurse he was having an affair with in the basement.

The building's current owner said that an unnamed local resident had driven up to him when he first purchased the building and referred to the location as "the Looney Bin," but neither I nor the director of the Madison Historical Society could find any records that there was anything but a positive outlook on the world conducted at the seminary. She had never heard the building called by that moniker.

A New Hypothesis

Despite our efforts, we couldn't validate any of the claims that the owner of the Madison Seminary had expressed about the evil happenings that had reportedly occurred there. In addition to that, we had come across a YouTube series he produced that depicted re-enactments of violent acts in the seminary where other individuals pretended to be patients and hospital staff. A recurring theme in these videos was the alleged abuse that patients endured, none of which was rooted in documented fact. All these facts coalesced into a single hypothesis: did we go into this investigation forcing a false narrative, as the building's owner had? Did this narrative upset any of the entities that may have been present? Or did we somehow manifest our own haunting?

We decided we'd enter the second night of the investigation with an open mind. During our run of the attic, armed with the recorded evidence of what occurred at Madison, we sat in the sweltering heat of the intimidating space, sigils and all, and started our line of questioning from scratch with an emphasis on respect. We asked several times if there were any entities present in addition to our investigative group. We were met with quiet and no feelings of agitation or dread.

We persisted with our line of questioning, our questions echoing back at us from the creaky wooden floors of the attic. Seated on the floor, staring at the Data Logger on the wicker wheelchair in front of us, it became difficult to stay awake. Spoiled by the excitement of the previous night, we became acquainted with the feeling most investigators come face to face with in their cases: boredom. The Data Logger registered a few temperature fluctuations, but we ignored them, given the natural drop in heat outdoors as the night progressed.

We stood up to combat the soporific effects of the lack of activity and redundant non-replies to our line of questioning. When we did, we heard noises emitting from the eastern side of the attic where several patient rooms were located. We stood still, thinking maybe our movement traveled through the wooden floor. That's when we heard it again. So we headed to the area, peering into every room and like the previous night, we began feeling there was a presence among us we couldn't quite put our finger on. Unlike last night's investigation, however, that sense of agitation or belligerence wasn't there. It was a feeling of acknowledgement.

We set our Data Logger on the floor along with our ambisonic microphone and began asking if there were any patients among us. Again, no environmental changes registered on our equipment, yet we continued to hear sounds of movement. So we shifted our focus onto the more positive aspects of Madison Seminary—to the women who were cared for there and the work that took place in the community. During our discussion of the more beneficial factors of the seminary, a single change in barometric pressure registered on our Data Logger. We watched the yellow light blink once, twice, then fade. All other attempts to communicate with the entities we believed we heard shuffling on the floor were met with absolute silence in the quiet attic.

Our Conclusion

The activity on night two was nothing like what we had experienced in the basement or what our other team members had endured in the same area. None of us had fallen ill or felt sick. As one member of the team commented, it felt "lighter" as we investigated.

What had become apparent to us is that our approach to the investigation had a significant effect on our findings. When we went in on the first night and attempted to push a narrative of abuse, it almost felt as if we were brushed off by the entities we were trying to contact. When we tried to communicate on a more personal, human level, we were met with an EVP of a woman's disembodied voice.

So is Madison Seminary haunted? If so, what kind of haunting took place there?

Mustafa: Let's go by the facts: there's no evidence, any where, no recorded documents, at all, to suggest the claims of abuse the women allegedly suffered at Madison Seminary is true. In fact, several documents the owner promised to procure for our team never came to light. Documents that would prove that antipsychotics and other drugs were nefariously administered to patients. Nor were they provided to our team during or after the investigation.

Paranormal tourism is big, big business. In fact, one of the first things the owner said to us when we arrived on the scene is that he "need[s] to make this [place] work," which set off alarms in my head. He talked about how he's dumped his entire life savings into owning and operating the building, and it was apparent to me how direly he needed the building to generate some kind of income. Then there were the videos that he and his team members uploaded to YouTube that constantly reinforced the more negative aspects of hauntings. I'd label this paranormal malpractice. I believe the entities there were sick and tired of a false narrative being tossed around without any historical basis. When we investigated and brought up the same old tired issues the client and his team have had on their ghost hunting runs, we were lashed out at, and rightfully so. Either that or the building's owner manifested the haunting they wanted to experience.

The combination of the lack of presented documentation, the owner's incessant reinforcement of a dark and evil narrative, and the strange sigils strategically placed throughout the building leads me to believe he's forcing some type of macabre aura that simply wasn't part of the Madison Seminary's history.

What I find tragic is that the building could remain a cultural fixture in Madison County and serve as a location for the local historical society. It is entirely possible to preserve the history of the town and such a meaningful structure while still holding paranormal tours. It could be a means to maintain the site and make it "work" for the client and his team, as well as other community members who have been positively affected by it.

Is it haunted? I believe it could be, but I also believe the aggressive activity we encountered is in direct correlation to the owner's own machinations. He's manifesting his own haunting. I find it sad but also fascinating at the same time.

Brandon: After countless hours of historical research, multiple days of investigating, and a thorough analysis of the data collected, Madison Seminary seems to have a very unusual phenomena taking place within its walls. I do believe there are entities inhabiting this beautiful building. Yet the misleading information and possible magic being practiced at Madison has changed the way the phenomena takes place. Because of this clash of organic phenomena and manmade phenomena, we have to classify Madison Seminary as a Class Five: Pseudo Haunting. The discovery of the sigils and not finding out what their intention or purpose was has to be taken into account. I do not believe the rise in negative phenomena and the appearance of the sigils are a coincidence.

Madison Seminary will have to be further investigated to fully understand why and how the phenomena seems to be ever evolving.

— 7 —
LIVING IN A
HAUNTED HOTEL

Brandon: For many people, researching ghosts and hauntings is considered a hobby. But there are a select few that make it a part of their being, part of their existence. After losing my brothers, my entire life changed. I was driven to find answers about the possible existence of life after death. In 2013 I received a call from a very good friend of mine asking if I wanted to rent an apartment in one of the most notorious haunted hotels in Southern California. There is only one way to respond to a question like that. Absolutely! Living in a haunted hotel gave me an experience that fostered a close bond to the Original Springs Hotel case.

Suicide Apparition at Original Springs

• Okawville, Illinois. Investigated in 2019 on A&E's *Ghost Hunters*. (Season one, episode eight, "Suicide Hotel.")

Claims

- Long history of owners dying by suicide.

- Feelings of uneasiness.

- Footsteps heard in the hallway.

- Shadow figures walking through the halls.

- Figure of a woman seen in a mirror in the bar/dining area.

- Sense of dread.

- Sense one is being followed.

History

(For further reading on the Original Springs Hotel, check out the wonderful *Haunted Illinois* article,[35] as well as the website of the article's author: AmericanHauntingsInk.com.)

The image of the Original Springs Hotel as it stands today elicited two polarizing reactions from our team. One: "Why in the world is the building's owner, Mary Rennegarbe, so fascinated with this place?" Two: "It *really* must have been something special in its prime." We found that this duality is likely the key to understanding the significance this hotel carried for several of its owners.

A historical fixture in Okawville, Illinois, the more than 130-year-old hotel clearly showed signs of age. It's no secret that the area isn't ranking high on the list of tourist destinations, either. So was Mary's obsession with the place a healthy one? And do the purported paranormal claims, along with the hotel's dark history, have anything to do with her inability to give up a venture that her family strongly intimated is a lost cause?

---

35. Troy Taylor, "The Original Springs Hotel in Okawville, Illinois," Haunted Illinois, 2004, https://www.hauntedillinois.com/realhauntedplaces/original -springs-hotel.php.

Interestingly enough, the Original Springs Hotel didn't begin with a business plan or even the desire to provide lodging to weary travelers. In fact, and there's a level of biological poetry to this, the birth of the location begins in the rather mundane way all life more or less begins: with water.

Miraculous Water

In 1867, a large mineral spring was first discovered in Okawville, Illinois, by a local saddle and harness shop owner by the name of Rudolph. He needed to dig a well for his business, and did so without issue, filling up his tin pots. However, he noticed that after a while, the utensils started to leak and, at the recommendation of a local tinsmith, replaced his inferior tin items with copper ones.

Well, those copper containers started to leak too. Searching for answers as to why the heck this water was eating through his receptacles, word spread to locals about the curious water beneath their feet. It caught the attention of a local doctor who tested the water and saw it had a high mineral content. Word got out to a local merchant who was fascinated with the chemical makeup of the water and decided to put up $25 to get the water in the hands of a professor in St. Louis, Missouri, for additional testing. This professor discovered the spring water contained no fewer than eight different minerals, with a special abundance in iron. Reportedly, it had a similar mineral composition to the world-renowned Carlsbad Mineral Water Baths in Germany and Arkansas Hot Springs. However, Okawville's water didn't emerge from the earth steamy and bubbling.

The Okawville doctor wondered if this water could prove beneficial to a rheumatic patient of his. He had repeatedly tried, and failed, to treat the patient with other methods, but when he used the springs on his patient—voilà, almost instantaneously they were relieved of their symptoms. It wasn't long before folks from all over the small community fancied a dip in the mineral waters they had luckily built their humble town upon.

The first small bathhouse to capitalize on the excitement surrounding the water's ameliorative properties was established on September 16, 1868, with a few others cropping up shortly after. Okawville (at the time, called Bridgeport) was only composed of six hundred people and the hotels weren't designed to accommodate the large throngs of visitors who began pouring in once the St. Louis and Southeastern Railroad came to town.

Anna's Vision

Word of mouth about the "miracle water" in Okawville spread quickly, and the town soon became a hot spot for folks from all over looking to help relieve joint pain and rheumatism symptoms, clear up their acne and eczema, and in some cases, treat psoriasis. For Anna Schierbaum, the healing properties of the Okawville Mineral Springs were almost as immediate as the doctor's patient zero. She viewed it as a natural blessing from above. Described as a "hopeless invalid" who suffered from rheumatoid arthritis, Anna visited the waters in 1884 and claimed that a dip in them completely transformed her. She was so elated that this natural wonder changed her life for the better that she wanted to spread the joy of the springs' curative bounty to as many people as possible.

The saddlemaker, Rudolph, who is attributed as the first to discover the springs, wanted to build an enormous, three-story brick structure to help house the numerous guests pouring into Okawville. While he was able to gather enough resources to establish a smaller operation, he was never able to realize his real dream of the grand Mineral Springs Hotel until Anna got involved.

She had convinced her husband, Reverend J.F. Schierbaum, to combine a hotel, restaurant, and mineral springs spa into a grand one-stop shop on top of a naturally flowing water source, allowing travelers from near and far to soak up the glorious H_2O beneath them without ever having to stray far from its salubriousness. With help from Anna's husband and a group of other Evangelical German ministers, Rudolph's vision was finally coming to fruition. Plans were drafted and construction started right away; however, brick proved to be way too expensive. So instead it was built from wood, a design choice that contributed to the degradation of the structure over time.

> **Mustafa:** As a history nerd, I loved spending time in the Original Springs Hotel, but spending extended periods of time in the indoor pool area was unpleasant. The combination of the temperature-controlled chlorinated water and original wood construction didn't allow for the best ventilation. It was muggy and I found it difficult to breathe. Right off the bat I wondered if this had anything to do with the adverse feelings visitors and employees had in the hotel.

Anna's realization of Rudolph's dream proved to be a success; the Mineral Wells (now known as Original Springs) thrived when it opened its doors on May 28, 1885. In fact, it did so well that J.F. made the decision to expand the building in 1886.

The First Deaths Begin

As part of the expansion plan, a threshing machine was purchased for the hotel's engine house, but the second-hand machine exploded. It scalded J.F. along with two other men: C.L. Schulze and a man named Meier. The latter was so badly burned that he died from his wounds. The tragic event didn't stop the popularity of the hotel and it still persisted as an oft-frequented tourist destination, despite the other piggyback businesses that began cropping up in Okawville.

In 1890, however, J.F. Schierbaum sold the hotel to J.W. Schreiner, a man from St. Paul, Minnesota, who would later become Okawville's fire chief and mayor. He handed operations of the hotel to his brother W.A. Schreiner, who managed to grow the Mineral Wells' hotel business even more, establishing it as *the* getaway in the region. Business boomed until 1892, when a fire raged throughout the building, almost destroying it completely. The official cause of the blaze was attributed to an exploding lamp, but rumors began to circulate throughout the town that it was attempted arson. Someone with a grudge against the Mineral Wells' former owners, the Schierbaums, had spread coals all over the floor. Could it have been Rudolph who had secretly begrudged the hotel's success and someone else's profit from his idea?

The Mineral Wells was rebuilt by the Schreiners, who made the structure larger and, again, it was a resounding success in the years that followed its reopening. But for some reason, in 1900, W.A. sold the hotel back to the Schierbaums. While no reason was given for the sale, many believe it had something to do with the death of his brother J.W.

The hotel continued to grow, with additional rooms and updated amenities added each season. In 1904, Reverend Schierbaum passed away from a seemingly innocuous illness. Although J.F. was the owner and operator of the Original Springs, Anna had wholly dedicated her time to maintain and promote the business. She luxuriated as its new matriarch almost immediately. Maintaining its reputation as a prime hotspot in Okawville for the last seven years of her life, Anna passed away in 1911 from an unknown sickness she battled for two months.

Her son Ben Schierbaum worked as a hotel clerk for years and was intimately familiar with the way his mother operated it. It continued to thrive under his supervision, leaving the young man one of the wealthiest young business owners in Okawville. He married Alma Schulze (daughter of C.L., who was scalded in the engine room accident), but it wasn't long before the two began experiencing problems. Alma left Ben in 1916, right around the time the hotel closed its doors for the winter season. She disappeared, sending Ben on a three-day search for her. When he returned to the hotel, he went to Alma's parents' store across the street, but they didn't provide him with any answers to her whereabouts.

He walked through the doors of the hotel that night for the last time.

Five days after Ben's meeting with the Schulzes, a traveling salesman who was accidentally directed to the Original Springs while looking for a hotel entered the building. In search of anyone who could help him, he turned a corner into the hallway and noticed dried blood on the floor, along with the body of Ben Schierbaum. Half of his head was missing. A double-barrel shotgun was in his lap along with a note addressed to Alma's father, requesting he contact both the coroner and his brother Dan. Ben's final words asked C.L. to "forget the whole matter." Splayed on the ground were several other letters and photographs of Alma. Over a thousand people attended Ben's funeral. He was twenty-eight years old.

The Schierbaum's heirs owned and operated the hotel until 1919, until it changed ownership a couple of times. Some of the owners were more colorful than others. For example, the hotel was sold again in 1924 to a St. Louis corporation that operated it during America's bootlegging years. Known gangsters would spend time in the hotel, and shoot-outs even occurred right in front of the building. The violence was rumored to be directly related to the booze hidden under a trapdoor that led to a secret room in the hotel, but this was never confirmed.

In 1929, Conrad Paeben was put in charge of operating the hotel by the St. Louis business that owned it. He proposed several exciting new changes and renovations to the structure, many of which were never implemented, save for a few key ones. A steam-heating system was installed so the building could be open all year. He also had a penchant for promotion; he posted fliers wherever he could, took out radio ads, and even coined a catch phrase, calling the Original Springs (the hotel had gone through several name changes) the place "Where Rheumatism Meets its Waterloo." Despite the fact that America was undergoing a depression, Conrad was able to make the Original Springs' business model work for a short period of time. He sold country club memberships, updated the building's interior with new decor, renovated its bathhouse, and added a miniature golf course. Larger plans to add tennis courts and a full-sized golf course, however, never came to fruition.

Primarily due to the Great Depression, plans to turn the Original Springs Hotel into a full-blown country club were fiscally unrealistic, so the name was changed to the Original Springs Health Resort. And still, business suffered direly. Despondent and broke, Conrad Paeben poisoned himself in 1933, making him the second owner of the hotel to die by suicide.

It seemed like the Original Springs would close for good, but it received an unexpected third wind thanks to Tom Rogers, who worked at the Original Springs in 1931. He transformed the Original Springs into a social club and held Democratic Party gatherings there. Nightly forty-five-cent unlimited beer passes kept guests coming in to watch the orchestras and bands perform and kept people participating in local dances and festivities. Even though the Depression had adversely affected not only the hotel, but Okawville as a whole, Tom was able to counter by diversifying his business model. He urged local farmers to produce more grade C milk, which was perfect for processing cheese but not drinking. Farms began cropping up in the area, all under the Original Springs Banner. But his fascination with dairy, and eventually hog farming, overtook his interests in running a hotel. The Original Springs saw huge numbers on the weekends but had almost no visitors from Monday through Thursday. Tom was still the owner of the hotel as World War II hit, and because most Americans were focused on the war effort and generally stayed closer to their own homes and neighborhoods, many sections of the Original Springs Hotel were closed off to guests.

As the years progressed, Tom became more and more of an isolationist and opted to spend time on the farms he managed, until they, too, were no longer of interest to him. He had given up on promoting both the hotel and his farming businesses, the bulk of which ceased operations in 1953. The final years of Tom's life saw him aimlessly walking around the hotel, greeting the few guests who came from time to time, but he mostly kept to himself. On a March morning in 1962, Tom was found dead in one of the upstairs hotel rooms while the building was closed—cause of death unknown. Some believe that senility and/or dementia may have contributed to his passing. A capable man with a strong work ethic once brimming with hope and passion, Tom too had died in the hotel. No heir could be found for months and his estate was sold in 1962 to Albert and Doris Krohne.

The Krohnes got to work immediately updating the Original Springs, but a head-on truck collision left Albert, a carpenter, unable to perform many of the planned renovations for the building, stymying the couple's plans. The Krohnes sold it in 1974 to Robert and John Scrage, who tapped out after two years and sold it back to Albert and his wife.

The Krohnes were able to run the hotel with middling success and although they managed to implement some of their original renovation plans, major ones were met with disaster. A mechanical apparatus to open the roof of the building that housed the pool never worked quite right. To make matters worse, in 1988 a defective electrical outlet in the bar area started a fire that resulted in some $400,000 worth of damage, which was exacerbated by firefighters having to knock out windows and tear down walls to control the blaze. The flames were a blessing in disguise, as the necessary demolition helped make space for larger rooms and a restructuring of the hotel's interior.

The Krohnes sold the Original Springs Hotel to Mary and Don Rennegarbe in 1990. Mary started working at the hotel in 1979 as a waitress and it was her longtime dream to one day be its owner, a dream that came to fruition like so many before her. But like the hotel's former owners, would it soon become a source of frustration and despair, if it hasn't already?

The Living

- Mary's family calls *Ghost Hunters* to come in and look into the paranormal claims of the building.

• Will Mary end up like the hotel's previous owners, given the history of suicide?

The Dead

• If there is indeed paranormal activity occurring in the "Suicide Hotel," could it be linked to the following former owners?

  • Anna Schierbaum

  • Ben Schierbaum

  • Conrad Paeben

  • Tom Rogers

• If there is an owner wandering the halls, do they want to have anything to do with Mary?

Investigation

Seeing the Original Springs Hotel for the first time, it was difficult to not imagine what it looked like in its heyday. What we were presented with was a sad reminder of what happens to so many once-bustling American towns.

Even though the wooden structure was in dire need of a paint job, it still maintained some of its older charm, but it was apparent that this business had seen better days. Keeping in mind its dark history, plus the general feeling of desolation and abandonment in the town, we wondered what exactly was keeping Mary tied to this location. Was she the kind of headstrong woman that Anna was? If this was the case, and there was an entity that was following people throughout the location, we wondered if Anna's ghost was following Mary around because the two shared a common passion.

History is cyclical, and in the case of the Original Springs Hotel, it's a repeated history that many people would avoid. With multiple owners dying by suicide, Mary's family expressed their worries that her obsession with the location could be linked to some type of inimical paranormal influence. Would Mary end up like Ben? Like Conrad Paeben? Or Tom Rogers, so full of hope and energy to promote the hotel and make it work, but slowly seemed to lose his mind to apathy? Could her stubbornness to make the Original Springs Hotel a successful business have been inherited from the hotel's second owner? An owner who fell on hard financial times and persistently toiled to reclaim his fortune, but to no avail. Did she have horse blinders on, so to speak? Because she was seemingly possessed by a harmful entity's own willingness to fit a square peg in a round hole? The concern from her family was palpable. There have been many Hollywood horror stories that were based on occurrences just like the one Mary's family feared was occurring right before their eyes. They felt powerless to stop it so decided to call us to see if there was any truth to the paranormal claims, and also perhaps talk some sense into their mom and convince her to stop dedicating her life to a business venture that was, to put it politely, an uphill battle.

It's All in the Mind

Before we even stepped foot into the hotel's massive wooden structure, our previous experiences had our minds buzzing with variables to consider. Chief among them was whether or not the water the hotel was built on was somehow responsible for the alleged paranormal occurrences going on there. There is a long-standing theory in the paranormal world that running water is a conduit for ghostly activity, and we speculated that its mineral-heavy content may be of some consequence as well.

We always start on earth, so to speak, so we immediately searched for possible natural elements in the hotel that could play with people's minds. As is the case with many old buildings that have been updated to meet modern requirements, the Original Springs Hotel could very well have a bleeding EMF issue. Older wiring systems are known to not have the best insulation, so we heavily considered that ahead of our work.

You may be asking yourself, "What does old wiring have to do with ghosts?" Well, nothing, but possibly everything. In many similar instances, buildings that need proper electrical work will leak electromagnetic frequencies into the air, and this could have a significant effect on temporal lobe activity (not to mention possibly contributing to false positives on EMF detectors).

Some individuals are more sensitive to electromagnetic frequencies, which could possibly instill or even implant feelings of dread or similar scary sensations the employees and hotel visitors had reported. There was also the question of infrasound, or ultralow frequencies that, while undetectable by the naked ear, have significant effects on an individual's mental state. It was imperative that we first test the possibility that all of the ominous feelings—the sensation of being watched or followed, and the fear of something lurking around every corner—could be directly attributed to natural phenomena: namely EMF adversely affecting people's temporal lobes.

It Starts with Ben

Being *Ghost Hunters*, it was a tantalizing prospect to entertain the notion that some of the suicides that occurred in this building could be responsible for some of the activity that was being reported, so one of the first areas of the hotel that we investigated was the hallway where Ben Schierbaum had died by suicide.

Mustafa: This was a touchy case for both Brandon and me, and I wanted to make sure the two of us kept our wits about us while we investigated. I attempted suicide at one of the lowest points in my life, and by complete happenstance survived.

Brandon sadly lost a brother to suicide, and I wanted to make sure I was being respectful to not only any entities that might still be lingering in the Original Springs Hotel who tragically took their lives, but also the memory of Brandon's brother, as well as Brandon's mental state. I'm not going to lie. Going into this investigation, a part of me worried that if any paranormal activity occurred, it might adversely affect either Brandon or me due to our associated histories with suicide.

Brandon: Losing a brother to suicide made this a very personal case. Not to mention the experience I had losing a friend to suicide at the hotel where I lived for almost three years. When developing the classification system, I knew that there were similar phenomena throughout the world. I had no idea that certain buildings would almost mimic one another. This investigation would be a true test for the classification system and how it would be implemented in the field.

We walked into the hallway where Ben's body was found. In the darkness of the Original Springs Hotel, our feet thudding on its old carpet stretched over its old wood, we began our first portion of the investigation. Although it was clear the hallway showed the building's age, it was still hard to shake the idea that the hotel must've really been a sight to behold back when Anna and Ben or even Conrad or Tom ran the place.

We brought an EDI+ Data Logger along with audio recording equipment for our coverage of the hallway and immediately performed an EMF sweep. We noticed that some areas of the hallway contained abnormally high levels of EMF, namely one specific location on the floor. Now some individuals may jump the gun and believe it could be directly attributed to paranormal activity. After all, this is the hallway where Ben killed himself, so there's a temptation for some gung-ho investigators to claim that the electromagnetic frequencies being registered by our devices were caused by the ghost of Ben Schierbaum. But the fact that the EMF was so sustained and measured immediately ruled out that possibility. It was clear that there was wiring underneath the floor that led to certain parts of the hotel, and it was concentrated in this area.

What's more is that a separate investigation conducted in the restaurant confirmed that this was indeed the case. The EMF was so high in that specific area that we could document it from the floor below. As far as we were concerned, anyone sensitive to electromagnetic frequencies would be adversely affected after prolonged exposure. Even we felt somewhat anxious during the course of our investigation. We believe this was a direct result of being exposed to such high levels of EMF for sustained periods of time. Or, on a more basic level, we walked through a spooky-looking historical hotel with a history of suicide, actively looking to document paranormal activity. For the most part, Ben's hallway seemed to have more practically explicable phenomenon taking place than anything ghostly.

Unexplained Phenomenon

After finding an area that was devoid of EMF contamination farther down the hallway, we set our Data Logger down and began to ask if there was anyone present. The hallway was quiet and dark, with no indicators on our device suggesting any environmental changes had taken place. Just the familiar glow of the orange lights reading the temperature of a warm summer evening.

As we discussed the history of the hotel and Mary's family's concern for her workaholism, two yellow flashes permeated the night. Our Data Logger had recorded changes in barometric pressure. Was there something we said that resonated with an entity? We asked if anyone was attempting to communicate with us and welcomed them to interact with the device again.

Nothing.

We began repeating our topics of conversation earlier, discussing Ben, Mary, Anna, and other facets of the Original Spring's history.

Nothing.

Try as we might, we couldn't establish a consistent back-and-forth question/response protocol with any possible entities. So what caused those changes in barometric pressure? We had no idea, but it was becoming evident that our investigative work in Ben's hallway was, at least at the moment, not presenting any possible paranormal outcomes.

It was then we decided to explore other rooms in the hotel on the same floor. Perhaps that pressure change was actually an entity walking through the hallway and into another area. We walked through several old wooden doors into different rooms. The stark contrast between old fixtures and stylings with modern appliances was visible, even in the darkness. But there was no abnormal activity to speak of; just high, sustained EMF spikes in specific areas. These were again attributed to electromagnetic frequencies not being insulated enough from both the wiring and different pieces of tech located on the premises.

There's Something on the Third Floor

Satisfied we had the beginnings of a logical explanation for those who experienced feelings of dread on the main floor, we decided to continue our investigation to the floor above us, where Tom Rogers's body was reportedly found. We openly discussed the man's eccentricities and how his final days were bizarre by all accounts as we walked up the exit stairwell, the suffocating pool area not far from us. The third floor, design wise, was very similar to the floor beneath us. The light-colored paint cracked in some areas, and a well-worn carpet was beneath our feet. And sound-carrying old wood surrounded us, necessitating our need for stillness throughout our investigation.

Doing our best to minimize movement, we approached the end of the hallway where a singular piece of furniture stood tall: a hybrid dresser/vanity with a mirror. We placed our Data Logger on this piece of furniture and stepped back. We soon took note of the different vibe in this area.

While the floor was nearly identical to Ben's hallway, the feeling was much different. There was a heaviness in the air that paranormal investigators often discuss; it's as if the air is thicker, and a tingling begins to buzz on the back of one's neck. This could very well be a consequence of investigating in the dark and we were simply experiencing a carried-over ancient mammalian instinct. Or we were merely feeling the heat of the building traveling up to where we were on the third floor, something our Data Logger registered after we had settled into our investigation.

Soon we'd discover there may have been something more to the heavy feelings we first felt when we walked into the area.

The third floor was one of the areas where witnesses reported hearing footsteps. We decided to conduct an experiment: Mary's family members said they heard these footsteps shortly after she spent time on the floor. So we decided to re-create Mary's steps by carefully walking down to the end of the hallway as she would. Unlike Mary, who was too busy maintaining the hotel, we tried to directly address any entities that may be present, giving our Data Logger at the end of the hallway plenty of space for any entities that may be there to interact with it.

We mainly wanted to see if we could hear any of the footsteps that might potentially follow us as they'd reportedly followed Mary in the past. We waited, in the heat, straining our ears to hear anything past our controlled breathing. But there were no footsteps. We tried the experiment again.

We were met with more quiet.

We discussed practical reasons behind why people may have heard footsteps, including the age of the building and the fact it was constructed entirely out of wood. It also didn't help matters that the Original Springs was erected directly above a spring. Wood rots over time, especially when it's subjected to a running water source over the course of 130-plus years. Although some upkeep and renovations were performed on the Original Springs Hotel during this time, it wasn't generating enough income for a major overhaul. It's normal for creaks, pops, and traveling noises to occur in older wooden structures. Now, had the building been made of brick as Rudolph had initially intended, the noises, creaks, and alleged footsteps reported by workers and visitors might be a different story. But at the start of this particular run, any noises we heard we directly attributed to the building's age.

Looking down the empty halls at the motionless Data Logger, we again attempted to reach out to any entities that may possibly be there. Although there seemed to be nothing in those cream-colored walls aside from two paranormal investigators and a cameraman, we persisted with asking questions and encouraged any entities that may be trying to talk to us to repeat themselves, as we now had devices recording that may pick up what they were saying.

We went through our talking points, yet again, and the emotional connection that Mary must have to the building in order to work in it so assiduously. That's when the familiar yellow emanations flashed from our Data Logger—pressure changes. We looked at each other and held our breath. Were we on to something? Or were we experiencing yet another singular aberration like we did on the floor beneath us?

We encouraged each other to talk more about Mary but didn't directly address a particular entity or try to establish contact. Instead we discussed Mary's love for her work, her love for the building, and made that correlation between Anna's own passion for the hotel. The mention of Mary in tandem with Anna resulted in even more pressure changes on our Data Logger. We looked at each other in amazement. As spooky as it was, it was hard not to smile.

We knew that while it was easy to write off the audible footsteps in the area, documenting pressure changes that seemed to react at the mention of the building's current and original owners—two women with enviable worth ethics, in an area that gave us the heebie-jeebies—was a bit more difficult to explain; especially because it occurred in an area with purported past claims of paranormal activity.

It's almost impossible to ascertain if we documented the presence of Anna or one of the hotel's other owners. This is primarily because we didn't document enough of a sustained response in pressure change when we shifted our conversation away from us and asked questions of the entity that could have possibly caused those pressure changes. But were those shifts in pressure caused by a ghost? Again, it's difficult to say, but we did find the little data we gathered compelling, and there was always audio to review. Not to mention the crazy episode members of our crew experienced while filming supplemental footage (B-roll).

Offending the Entities?

What intrigued us about this possible haunting is that witnesses claimed they spotted a woman wearing clothing from the early 1900s traversing the hallway. It's a commonplace claim, but one we took seriously nonetheless and left 4K lockoff cameras fixated on this area during the investigation, as well as bringing FLIR thermal imaging cameras on our runs in the area.

While we weren't able to capture any evidence of this apparition, while shooting B-roll footage, our camera crew reportedly captured an image of someone running toward them at the end of the hallway.[36] This occurred on the second floor where Ben Schierbaum shot himself in the head. We theorize that if the captured entity is actual evidence of a paranormal occurrence, then the controversial circumstances leading up to this incredible visualization may have had something to do with its materialization.

---

36. "Haunted Hotel," @GhostHunters, Instagram, September 26, 2019.

As we discovered at the Madison Seminary, focusing on negative narratives, whether steeped in historical fact or not, can sometimes drum up paranormal activity.

While we reviewed audio and video from our runs back at the hotel, crew members excitedly contacted the team to alert them of the find on the B-roll footage. We pressed them for details, and one of our production managers, still sweating and wide-eyed thinking about the incident, described how they were standing in the location as the re-creation was being shot. That's when they felt an invisible force rush through them—as if something had passed through their bodies. Then he presented us with the captured image: the visual was intriguing. At the end of the yawning hallway appeared to be a large figure with a round face lumbering toward the camera. To call it unsettling would be an understatement and any attempts to re-create it were unsuccessful.

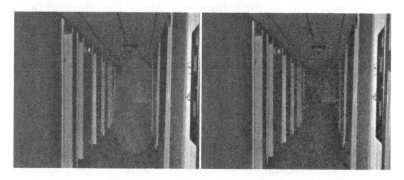

Hallway entity at Original Springs Hotel.

This image gathered from our crew was discovered after they re-created the scene of Ben taking his own life for this episode. We theorized that if there was indeed an entity in that image, then it may have been angered and/or triggered by our re-enactment of such a horrific moment. Ben Schierbaum's decision to end his life occurred at the most vulnerable time in his life, and we postulated that perhaps our re-creation was either deemed insensitive, or it somehow tapped into that moment.

That sense of loss is nothing to be trifled with, and visually toying with a person's feeling that any chance of happiness was forever robbed from them, so much so they were compelled to take their own life, made us think that an entity may have lashed out in anger as a result. It's just a theory, but it's very interesting that the only visual evidence we gathered at the hotel occurred when we filmed this re-creation, and in the same location Ben took his life.

Another segment of one of our other runs in the Original Springs started to pique our interest during the evidence review process as well. During our run of the third floor, we couldn't resist leaving the eerie hallway and spending some time in the even eerier room where Conrad Paeben had reportedly poisoned himself. Just outside that room, in the hallway, was where Tom Rogers's body was found. Although we didn't notice it in the moment as our eyes darted around the darkness while listening for footsteps, our handheld camera picked up pressure change registrations on our Data Logger. It was like watching footage from the climactic scene of a horror movie, except we shot it ourselves in less than sixteen hours and it had actually happened.

We had referenced Tom Rogers and how he met a tragic end at this location and then boom: two pressure changes registered on the Data Logger. When we tried to further pursue that line of questioning, we didn't encounter any more activity on our Data Logger. However, when our attention was drawn by a question from a member of our production team, our handheld camera captured more pressure changes as we talked about Tom Rogers and Conrad Paeben with a producer who asked us if their deaths were confirmed suicides. We said we weren't 100 percent sure, but both men were found dead on the premises. The entire time we spoke about Conrad and Tom, pressure changes registered on the Data Logger. When we commenced our investigation and asked questions pertaining to Ben Schierbaum and Mary, there were no pressure changes to speak of.

Infrasound

One of the scariest claims we wanted to get to the bottom of was the ghost in the antique mirror in the lower-level dining/bar area of the hotel. We walked through the wooden hallways, OmniMic and laptop in hand, and down the stairs into the pool area. The smell of chlorine and the thick humidity luxuriating in the timber planking of the pool area accosted us before we even made it into the restaurant. Looking at the single, small ventilation shaft, it became clear why previous owners had wanted to create a retractable awning; the air was oppressive. We thought this stifling atmosphere may have contributed to the feelings of unease some visitors, guests, and employees had experienced at the Original Springs.

The wooziness was difficult to shake as we set up our infrasound test among the tables and chairs of the eatery. We also noticed there were fewer sounds coming from the floor of this lower level, maybe by virtue of this portion of the building resting on a foundation. There were also the thick, patterned carpets to consider. There had been plenty of mentions of footsteps in other parts of the building, but no audible claims in the basement.

First we wanted to ascertain whether or not there was any infrasound in the restaurant area, as we did in Grandma's Attic in our Athenaeum investigation. We fired up the program and sat in silence, watching the ambient noise levels on our graph. The frequency was well below that of conscious human hearing, but we had to monitor the decibel level of this low-frequency noise that eluded our ears, at least superficially. Sure enough, in addition to the high levels of easily explained EMF activity, we also recorded high levels of infrasound.

We kept the mic running for a few minutes and discovered a sustained infrasound frequency that would be just unnerving enough to trigger some people's senses and make them uneasy. It would have been interesting to see a dog's reaction to that space, as their ears would surely pick up noises. What's more is that we recorded some of the highest infrasound levels near the area where witnesses claimed to see an apparition manifesting itself in an antique mirror.

Next, we needed to see if we could re-create the circumstances surrounding the claim. We measured the distance in which witnesses saw the apparition. At the time, we conducted this experiment at night. However, we repeated it during the day to be as thorough as possible.

We tried to position ourselves throughout the room to see if there was any angle in which one could quickly look in the mirror and perceive a reflection that shouldn't be there. And there were. When one stood far enough away from the mirror, it wouldn't reflect an entirely accurate facsimile of its surrounding. The mirror was a bit warped, so when one stood far away from it, it was easy to see how one could mistake a piece of furniture, or even their own reflection, as an amorphous or ghostly figure.

To see if there were further explanations for individuals perceiving someone or something in the mirror, we walked outside to see if a shadow could be cast on the mirror through the Original Springs Hotel's windows. We came to the conclusion that someone could see a "spooky" image in the mirror if it was a reflection of someone in another part of the room, or if they were at a particular distance from the mirror.

Once we were able to successfully re-create the ghostly visage in the mirror, it was time to investigate behind the bar. And no, we didn't tap the keg for research purposes (as much as we wanted to), but we did have a laugh about it. That is until the EMF detector on our Data Logger flooded the room with blue light, registering a huge spike in electromagnetic frequencies.

We grabbed the Data Logger and watched the EMF drop down and then spike up again. This seemed to be aberrant activity, so we decided to set down the device and see if there was an entity attempting to communicate with us. Did it like our beer joke? We repeated it and asked if there was anyone else there who wanted a drink. The lights on the Data Logger again emanated and we saw numerical increases in EMF, which then dropped back down.

So there was an increase when we mentioned beer! Great! It made sense for a ghost bar fly to hang out near booze. But after looking at the Data Logger, we noticed there was another increase, even when we were silent. Then we asked if there was someone with us and if they could be so kind as to confirm their presence. The EMF spiked again before we could complete our sentence.

The more we watched the Data Logger, the more it seemed like the EMF levels were patterned. There would be a slight lull in EMF that then shot up every few minutes. We knew it couldn't be the batteries in the device as we swap them out before every run. We troubleshot it the best way possible: by turning it off and back on. But there was no change; still consistent low EMF bounces, punctuated by sudden increases, then right back down to a lull.

That's when we decided to move the Data Logger to see if it was resting near an old power line that might not have the same quality insulation as modern electrical systems. And while we were disappointed that we weren't going to be knocking back any crispy boys with a phantasm, we were happy to get to the bottom of the strange EMF behavior: wiring. We set the Data Logger on a table right underneath a power line that was in the ceiling. The same line that was in the hallway where Ben Schierbaum's body was found.

We continued our investigation in the kitchen. Again we only registered EMF and no other environmental changes. And all of the EMF we encountered was linked to an electrical source or activated appliance.

For the bar/restaurant area, we concluded that the feelings of dread were more than likely attributed to the high EMF levels we registered in the area, combined with the high levels of infrasound (ultralow frequencies) that could be adversely affecting temporal lobe activity. The creepy feelings one may encounter with these amalgamated elements could easily make someone feel like they saw a ghost in a mirror when it was probably just a misshapen reflection of themselves. Once all of these factors were added together, we were pretty convinced there was nothing paranormal going on in this area. Especially because we hadn't captured any ghostly evidence whatsoever.

There's also one other very important factor to consider: the restaurant was located very close to the source of the Original Springs spring water itself, not just the pool. In fact, in a room adjacent to the bar, all one had to do to gain access to the actual springs was lift up a piece of the floor and walk a few feet down to submerge themselves in the highly conductive mineral spring water, but more on that later.

The Haunted Spa

The spa area looked like the perfect location for a scene in a slasher flick. To access it, we had to walk through the thick air of the muggy pool area again and up an exposed stairwell with a walkable overpass. We made our way to the end of the hall and up some more stairs until we were finally greeted with the faded white decor of the spa. The stacks of white linens glowed in the dark night of the room, an effect magnified by the spa's blacked-out windows. Compartmentalized lockers, massage rooms, and spa chairs punctuated the old decor and contributed to the overall creep factor of the area.

The spa was closest to the third floor of the building, which is the area where we experienced significant paranormal activity. We set down our Data Logger and asked if there was anyone there with us, and if there was, could they please reach out and interact with the device we just set down?

Again, blue lights emanated from the Data Logger. We were initially excited and began to thank whoever was there, which prompted more EMF responses. We then asked about the building's original owner, Anna, and again, EMF spikes. This was another area where employees and visitors reported feelings of dread. They felt as if they were being watched or weren't alone. Seeing our Data Logger register punctuated electromagnetic frequencies had us initially believing there was possibly some ghostly activity taking place.

We waited in silence and continued to watch our Data Logger register these electromagnetic frequencies. Was there an entity walking in the room without our knowledge? We attempted to conduct a session, and it appeared there was someone or something interacting with our device at the behest of our questions, but we noticed there was no method or consistency associated with the EMF spikes. In other investigations where we established contact with an entity, there was sometimes a learning curve on their behalf when using these devices to communicate with us. (Our case in Worley Hospital in Pampa, Texas, is clear evidence of this, which we delve into later in the book.)

However, we soon noticed there was a cyclical methodology to the EMF spikes we encountered. They first occurred in bursts and then disappeared altogether. And then every few minutes or so it would ramp up again. Why was this?

It turns out there was a perfectly logical explanation: the air conditioning unit. It periodically turned on and off, and when energy was supplied to the unit it caused our Data Logger to register EMF spikes due to the poor electrical insulation. This run was a great example as to why EMF sweeps are so vital before investigating. While some paranormal investigators may be tantalized to attribute this to paranormal activity, it would be irresponsible to ignore all of the other environmental factors surrounding this phenomenon.

The rest of our investigation in the spa yielded no strange findings, and evidence review on all audio and visual footage from this run coincided with our run-through.

Conductive Water

The Original Springs Hotel was aptly named after the water it was built upon. Like any good mystery, this obvious and simple fact turned out to be the key behind most of the paranormal reports circulating the location. After we conducted this next experiment, the explanation was quite simple in retrospect.

We tested the water's conductivity, and as it turns out, the motion of the springs' current wasn't an amplifier for paranormal occurrences. Instead, it bolstered the already strong electromagnetic frequencies bleeding from the hotel's wiring that were probably instilling visitors and employees with these feelings of dread and fright. The Original Springs' biggest issue wasn't its alleged ghosts; it was essentially a magnet that was messing with people's minds. Workers were so spooked that they didn't want to hold shifts in the building, so how could Mary expect to run her place of business? So what's the solution in this scenario? While not perfect, we did come up with a temporary solution that didn't necessitate costly renovations to the hotel: take periodic breaks to go outside and shake off any of the adverse effects of long-term exposure to electromagnetic frequencies and high levels of infrasound.

But this didn't solve the biggest issue that Mary's family had with her obsession with the Original Springs Hotel. Why was she wholeheartedly dedicating her life to running a business that would probably never see the same success it did in its heyday and was a source of tragedy for so many others?

While we did capture some compelling finds in the Original Springs Hotel, it's difficult to say that we definitively provided proof that there were entities attempting to ensnare Mary in some perpetual suicide pact that was passed down from owner to owner. We're big fans of *The Shining*, but we'd wager that this certainly wasn't the case with Mary's hotel.

Our Conclusion

Mustafa: As an outsider, it's easy to judge people who dump all of their time and resources into a fool's errand. But after meeting Mary, it was evident that she was happy with the work that she was doing; it was work that kept her youthful. When I first met Mary,

I actually thought she was her son's younger sister. I couldn't believe she gave birth to this man who reached out to us for help.

At the risk of sounding too philosophical, one could argue that everything we do in life, even if it's successful, is ultimately a failure. That's because life is finite; it ends. No matter what story we craft for ourselves, it all ends the same way: we die. Every single business venture, no matter how profitable, will eventually fold. Even the greatest civilizations will at some point be condensed and boiled down to a single chapter in a history book. Every single person, if we're lucky, will be buried by loved ones with our names engraved in stone. But here's Mary, dedicating herself to a venture that is, by all accounts, pointless. I don't foresee the Original Springs Hotel becoming a great tourist destination in Mary's lifetime, nor do I think that Okawville, Illinois, will suddenly become a city like Las Vegas or Manhattan. Mary has an obsession—one I don't understand—with running a business that makes her happy day in and day out. How many millionaires and billionaires are absolutely miserable? How many horrifying stories of success, fame, and fortune have we watched on late-night docuseries specials that end in tragedy? From rock stars, to actors, to the wealthiest of business people, many of them didn't think their lives were worth it. If Mary found an obsession, no matter how foolish and, quite frankly, downright stupid it seemed to members of her family and our team who visited the hotel, who are we to say that she isn't happy? Even though I suggested to her and Don that they should try to sell it to the state of Illinois as a historical landmark, I can't shake the feeling that Mary truly believes that she belongs there. She found an obsession that was worth it to her. I've come across so many people who are haunted, not only by paranormal entities, but the mistakes of their own past and the search for a more fulfilling life. Mary didn't come across that way to me. She seemed like she was exactly where she needed to be, and that's a feeling I'm not ashamed to admit I'm a bit jealous of.

Brandon: Because of the similarities between the hotel that I lived in and the Original Springs Hotel, I can't ignore the correlation between the phenomena. I believe the environmental conditions factor into the haunting. The high levels of EMF and infrasound at the Original Springs seem to amplify the activity.

Observing the way these buildings affect people has to be considered. I was lucky enough to have the opportunity to collect data at the Glen Tavern Inn for many years. This leads me to believe that we are dealing with a Class Three: Suicide Apparition. This case perfectly demonstrates how to implement the classification system and how this system will further the scientific aspect of the paranormal field.

— 8 —
VICTORIAN ERA HAUNTINGS

Ghosts and hauntings are more often than not associated with the Victorian Era. For many paranormal investigators, there is a level of romanticism in looking for souls of a bygone era. The Victorian Era's fascination with death changed the way most Americans deal with death and the afterlife.

Death in America changed during the Civil War. Because of the massive number of casualties, the way the dead were cared for had to change, and so the funerary traditions and beliefs evolved. It was at this time that many Americans changed their perception about ghosts and the afterlife. A series of superstitions were adopted. Family photographs were turned facedown to prevent possession by the dead. Mirrors were covered with black crepe to prevent the deceased's soul from getting trapped in the mirror.

It could very well be said that Victorian death culture created paranormal investigation as we know it.

In this chapter we will examine one of the most active Victorian homes in the United States. As with any case we investigate, the classification system provides us an insight into the correlation of these types of highly active locations. The Victoria Era belief system may play a part in the activity taking place in these types of locations. Does their mindset, their belief system, retain in death?

As we break down the family's history and their way of life, a clear pattern starts to emerge.

Familial Haunting at the Glenn House

- Cape Girardeau, Missouri. Investigated in 2019 on A&E's *Ghost Hunters*. (Season two, episode eight, "The Glenn Family Curse.")

Claims

- Loud banging from first-floor windows.
- A growl or scream near the first-floor window area.
- A bouncing ball sound upstairs.
- Random thumping heard throughout the home.
- Little footsteps from the children's room.
- Organ/piano playing by itself.
- The bell system rings by itself, even after it's disconnected.
- A man wearing a dark coat in the kitchen area.
- A woman peeking down the staircase.
- A woman wearing 1900s clothing on the front lawn.
- A woman looking outside from the upstairs window.
- 1900s-era coins thrown from out of nowhere.

• Guests touched on the shoulder by invisible hands.

• Security system motion triggers activating by themselves.

• Doors opening and closing on their own.

• Cellar door padlock unlocked on its own.

• Christmas gifts unwrapped by themselves at night.

• Lights turn on when there isn't any power.

• A cold spot occurs at the bottom of the staircase.

History

We'd like to extend our thanks to Sarah Glenn Marsh, who so generously shared her family's history with us, including Sally's letters and poems, and allowing their usage in this book.

Mustafa: What's in a name?

I'd say everything you stand for. Your actions and what you're known for. Your character. Your perception. And when I hear the name Glenn, I can't help but think of my own family. Of what we never had, then claimed, then lost, and are now fighting to regain again.

Brandon: Like many prominent Victorian families, the Glenns showed their wealth in multiple ways. David was fascinated with technology. The Glenn House, as it stood in 1883, was the equivalent to a modern-day smart home, lined with bell systems, Edison wiring, and other state-of-the-art home devices. This Victorian Era technology would play a part in some of the unexplained activity taking place in the home.

If you look out the windows of the Glenn House's top floor and peer out a few hundred feet, you'll see the Mississippi River, so close you can smell it from the home when it rains. Separating the land from the river is a large concrete levee of sorts that sits at the embankment. Right past the water is Illinois. A quick drive through the surrounding area in Cape Girardeau will show that while homes and buildings have been updated for the most part, city planners have managed to keep much of its personality intact. This can likely be directly attributed to their obvious love for the city's history. A history that David A. Glenn was very much a part of.

David moved to Cape Girardeau when he was nineteen years old with little to his name (around $25 in his pocket) and was able to secure gainful employment through his cousins A.D. and W.B. Leech, who owned a general merchandising business. In many ways, David's advancement in Cape Girardeau seems to mimic the city's history itself.

Cape Girardeau was a humble trading post that flourished throughout the years as it was a mercantile vantage point. Its most significant developments were precipitated after the invention of the steamboat in 1835, which helped turn the city into the highest-trafficked port in America, right up until the Civil War. Union general Ulysses S. Grant even established his headquarters in Cape Girardeau before moving to Cairo, Illinois. Miraculously, the city was left relatively untouched during the war and it continued to flourish after the Confederate secession was quelled in 1865. David Glenn arrived a few years later during a very interesting and profitable time in Cape Girardeau history.

A Booming Business

Most goods were still brought into Cape Girardeau via shipping vessels, and it would be another twenty-two years until a rail line was built to the city. Whether through fiscal luck, sharp business acumen, a staunch work ethic, being at the right place at the right time, or a combination of the aforementioned, David Glenn became an extremely successful businessman and a popular fixture in Cape Girardeau's community. He amassed a consequential amount of wealth, wealth he reportedly wasn't afraid to share with his community. David anonymously covered people's hospital bills and paid to pave roads in underserved parts of the city.

After establishing himself in the community, David became engaged to Lula Deane, daughter of renowned Kentucky-born architect Edwin Branch Deane, who is responsible for building several long-standing and celebrated Missourian buildings,[37] including the Glenn House. Construction on the Victorian-style home was completed in 1883, two years after David and Lula married. Interestingly enough, the home remained in Lula's name, which was not only highly unusual for the time period in which few women owned property, but also demonstrated how much Edwin cared for his daughter.

Lula and David quickly became a prominent duo of Cape Girardeau. They were a young and successful couple whose names held weight. They owned arguably the newest and most beautiful house in the area, and David's business ventures were not only flourishing financially but had become embedded into Cape Girardeau's community, which afforded David a certain amount of influence in the city. This made the Glenns people of consequence

---

37. "History of Cape Girardeau," City of Cape Girardeau, 2018, https://www .cityofcapegirardeau.org/about/history.

in Cape Girardeau, which is staggering when you think that only a few years prior, David first came to the city with nothing but the change in his pocket. David and Lula Glenn were so well regarded in Cape Girardeau that when President Howard Taft sailed down the Mississippi River, their daughter Ruth presented the commander in chief with a rose bouquet, which was a massive honor.

Much of David's early economic success could be attributed to the fortunes he amassed owning and operating the Glenn Mercantile Company, but the bulk of his cash flow stemmed from his position as president of the First National Bank. And while he extended his generosity to members of his community, he was also quick to extend that same largesse to his own family. The Glenn House underwent major renovations only a few years after it was built. A turret and verandah were added to the home, and it was outfitted with indoor plumbing and electricity, which was not only extremely luxurious for the time period, but also extremely expensive. The Glenns were also one of the first families to own telephones in Cape Girardeau; that's including businesses and official government buildings, a testament to David Glenn's desire to be on the forefront at all times. They were indeed the Joneses to keep up with.

A Series of Family Tragedies

Although the Glenns enjoyed a surfeit of economic success, their personal lives were unfortunately rife with sadness early on. Illness claimed the lives of three of David and Lula's children. A year after they married, their firstborn son, Henry, died at only six months old. Their second child, a daughter named Virgil, died at eighteen months in 1884. In 1847 another son, David E., passed away when he was only two years old. During this time period influenza and pneumonia, enteritis and diarrhea, and tuberculosis were the three leading causes of illness-related deaths, with children under the age of five comprising 40 percent of these fatalities. The Glenns had six children total: the young Henry, Virgil, and David E. were survived by their siblings Ruth, Garrett, and Sarah Sally Glenn who all lived into adulthood.

The five surviving members of the Glenn family, sadly, experienced a quick reversal of fortunes in the early 1900s. The First National Bank that David Glenn owned went under in 1914. Although he was president, the bank's daily operations were left to cashier L.S. Joseph, who allegedly made several poor loan decisions and attempted to mask his mistakes. Joseph vanished from town, leaving David to clean up the mess, who brought in bank examiners after learning of the issue. Since there wasn't any FDIC insurance in those days to protect both customers and the bank should anything happen in circumstances like this, stockholders were expected to cover double of what they had invested. Since David Glenn and the now derelict Joseph were the primary investors, David Glenn had to declare bankruptcy to cover this cost.

The Glenns had other business ventures to rely on, but their bankruptcy and loss of revenue from the First National Bank, plus the enormous financial toll it took on their family, made it difficult for them to fully recuperate. On August 22, 1914, the Glenn family house was sold at an auction in the courthouse square. A house designed by Lula's father and the location of his funeral, a house that saw the death of three Glenn children, a home that that was a symbol of pride for the man who moved to Cape Girardeau with nothing in his pockets, a home that housed one of the most prominent families in the area. No Glenn came to own or live in the house again in the years that followed.

The Glenns moved to 313 Independence Street after the bankruptcy and David opened up the D.A. Glenn Dry Good Store at an address that's still listed in Cape Girardeau today: 31 North Main Street. Although it was a downgrade in operational scale when compared to Glenn Mercantile, it was still a viable source of income. That is until 1922 when it caught fire and burned to the ground while David attended a baseball game. With nothing tying them to Cape Girardeau any longer, David and Lula sold their home and moved to Texas to join their son Garrett, who owned and operated a men's clothing store.

As for the Glenn House, several people lived in the home following its auction, including a doctor who treated some of his patients there, but the last residents it belonged to were the Erlbachers. "The family purchased the house because it was in very bad shape; [and] they were fond of [it]," according to Christy Mershon, the Glenn House's current director. After living in the home and performing a number of renovations to help maintain its original aesthetic, the Erlbachers handed over the home's deed to the Historical Association of Great Cape Girardeau to be preserved for future generations. Today, the Glenn House sits on the National Register of Historic Sites.[38]

The Letters of Sally Glenn

Today the Glenn House not only contains several original items that belonged to David Glenn's family, but also a sizable collection of written correspondence and poems from David and Lula's youngest daughter, Sarah, who went by Sally. It seemed from her letters that her personality was incongruous to the time period

---

38. DNR.MO.GOV, National Register of Historic Places Inventory Nomination Form, 1978, 1979.

and area in which she lived. Sally was a free spirit who dreamed of becoming a Hollywood actress, a desire that moved her out west from her native Missouri. Her letters contained poems where she candidly spoke of her romantic relationships, her self-admitted capricious nature, and her career aspirations in entertainment.

She tied the knot with a man by the name of Norman L. Hely in 1917 when she was eighteen years old. They had a child, Edward Glenn Hely, who unfortunately passed away when he was only ten days old. Interestingly, Edward carried the Glenn name, a strong indicator that the Glenns were still respected in Missouri and Sally was proud of her maiden name.

Sally eventually divorced Norman in 1924 before moving to California and marrying Donald M. McRae a year later in Los Angeles, but the date of their divorce is unknown. It was during this time period that Sally pursued her dream of becoming a Hollywood actress. A favorite family story was that she was friends with famed silent actor Douglas Fairbanks. After her divorce, Sally moved to Louisville, Kentucky, and married James B. Williams, with whom she had a child named David. Tragically James died of a heart attack in the lobby of the Brown Hotel in 1941 when David was only five years old.

Sally then married John Totten and the two of them lived in Miami, Florida. Their marriage didn't last, but David remarked it may have had something to do with John wearing T-shirts in the house, which is something Sally complained about, being a woman of high society who had an affinity for finer things. She eventually moved in with her son David in Virginia after he married and had a son of his own. While living with them, Sally died by suicide, suffocating herself.

Mustafa: Sally was of great interest to our investigation, not just because of her surviving written correspondence and willingness to express herself in ways that weren't common of the time period, but because of the personal connection her surviving great-granddaughter felt toward her.

Sally's only surviving son, David Williams, is the grandfather of author Sarah Glenn Marsh (named after Sarah, aka Sally), who came upon the Glenn House by sheer coincidence. On approximately May 3, 2014 (a date we believe to hold some significance), while looking through family photos, she saw a photograph of her great-great-grandfather, David Glenn. She noticed there was something written on the back of the photo: an address. She searched the address online and one of the first results was a Facebook page for the Glenn House. Sarah became suddenly privy to an entire chapter in her family's history she had never known before. What we find interesting is that a century after the Glenns had first declared bankruptcy and auctioned off their historic home, never to reside in it again, Sarah learned of its existence. It was almost one hundred years to the day. And it transpired by pure happenstance.

Sarah reached out to Christy (the director of the Glenn House) and arranged a visit to the home of her recent ancestors on October 12, 2014, curious to explore a building that meant so much to David Glenn and Cape Girardeau. After an emotional stay in which she shared some of her own Glenn family stories and saw such an important symbol of her lineage firsthand, Sarah left home for Virginia.

And that's when Christy first started experiencing paranormal activity in the Glenn House.

Shortly after Sarah's departure, the bell system in the house malfunctioned, sporadically going off without warning. It was so jarring and frightening to Christy that she called her husband to come and sever the wiring, not knowing how to fix it. Volunteers and visitors to the building reported being touched by invisible hands, and even claimed to have seen a man in a dark coat. The activity was so persistent that the Glenn House lost several volunteers, threatening the viability of the building as a historic tourist site.

Though the hauntings went on for years, Christy hadn't made the correlation between Sarah's first visit to the Glenn House and the ghostly occurrences she and her staff encountered. Occurrences that were exacerbated in intensity and frequency once Sarah returned in 2019.

It wasn't until another follow-up visit from Sarah that Christy began to suspect this particular Glenn descendant had something to do with the hauntings. The ramped-up activity saw doors in the home opening and closing by themselves in the middle of the night. Motion detectors would go off, despite there being nothing physically present to trigger them, and reports of footsteps stalking around the building while guests and volunteers traversed the premises became increasingly common.

Christy reached out to our team to discover if there was a logical explanation for the activity going on in the Glenn House and if Sarah had anything to do with what she and her staff were experiencing.

The Living

- Christy Mershon, board president of the Historical Association of Greater Cape Girardeau. She was admittedly shaken with the paranormal activity frightening not only her, but

her volunteers. Many of these staffers were so shaken by
the activity that they refused to return to the Glenn House.
Additionally we wanted to determine the nature of the activity, if there was any, as best as we could. Christy seemed convinced that it was negative and sad. What could cause this
permeating feeling of grief throughout the home?

• Sarah Glenn Marsh, author and living descendant of the Glenn
family. Did her appearance at the home heighten paranormal
activity that laid dormant there? Or did she bring said spirits
with her?

The Dead

• If there were spirits of the Glenn family living in the home,
was it the elder David A. Glenn? His wife Lula?

• Three of David and Lula's babies, Henry, Virgil, and David
E. Glenn, all died in the house. They were aged two years
or younger.

• Sarah Sally Glenn: while she didn't die in the home, she was
born into the better years of the Glenn family's affluence.
Did she miss the status that came with the home?

• If Glenn family spirits are indeed becoming more active after
Sarah Glenn Marsh's visits, we were open to the idea that it
may have to do with their relationship with Sally, seeing as
they share a name and as the Glenn descendant says herself,
some type of unspoken familial connection. Could this have
anything to do with the reported claims at the Glenn House?

Investigation

Mustafa: Ambivalent. It's the only way I can describe how I felt before heading into the Glenn House to investigate. Knowing what I knew about the Glenn family's tragic history, and the fact that they lost their home, pushed my own family's history of financial insolvency and home foreclosure to the forefront of my mind. I wondered if my childhood house would become like the Glenns' after I passed. Would I carry that with me well after I died? I feared I would as the Glenns' story weighed heavily on me.

Brandon: When I initially met with Christy, I could sense how terrified she was of the house. When we first walked in there was a picture frame lying in the middle of the parlor floor. Christy began to tell us that this was a common occurrence in the parlor. With the same exact photo. Upon picking it up to inspect it, we noticed right away the photo was of David Glenn. There were multiple moments where Christy was on the verge of tears because she was very concerned about finding docents to help with tours and maintenance of the property. For the past few years, docents had such intense paranormal encounters in the house that it led to their resignations. This was one of Christy's biggest concerns.

As difficult as it was to lug our heavy equipment up the long, wide concrete stairwell to the statuesque Glenn House, as paranormal investigators it felt like we were returning home. Yes, the 136-year-old structure fit the bill for a haunted location, but it was grand, and Christy had done a phenomenal job of maintaining its beauty.

We set up base in a carriage house in the backyard, which was pretty much a smaller home, before finally taking a tour of the historic location. It was adorned in dark, polished wood. The music room was filled with Glenn family heirlooms and period-appropriate items that transported us to the early 1900s. The stately furniture, expansive dining room, and molding on the ceilings and entranceways to each room screamed of classic American luxury.

Each step we took throughout the structure reminded us of the Glenn House's age; it was still an old home and while touring it we hypothesized that a variety of the paranormal claims could be directly attributed to the way it was constructed, structural shifts over the years, or even outdoor wildlife.

During our tour, we made note of the different creaks and croaks the wood made while we walked through the house. We were inclined to attribute a lot of the audio claims, like the thumping and little footsteps, to wood naturally expanding and contracting. We investigated during a particularly hot time in Cape Girardeau, and as the temperature dropped throughout the night, we wanted to ensure we considered this as a possible contributing factor for any strange noises. We made sure to keep this in mind during our runs.

Other claims also seemed to have completely practical explanations at first: the growl could be attributed to the litany of different wildlife nearby. We were right next to the Mississippi river after all.

Mustafa: While touring the location during the day, I spotted an otter a few hundred feet from the front of the house and excitedly tried to get a closer look at it. I'd never seen one in the wild before. It turns out the animals are common in Missouri, and I wondered if they could be responsible for the growl people heard near the front door, especially when they notoriously make a variety of strange noises. I was here not even a full day and one was ambling around not far from the Glenn House.

The feelings of being touched could be directly attributed to a draft, as could the cold spot on the bottom of the stairs. As for the bell system going off and the lights in the home turning on even when there wasn't any power, we planned to hire an electrician to take a look and let us know if there was anything wrong with the home's wiring.

As for the visual apparition sightings, the home is decorated with many windows, and although it wasn't located on an extremely busy street, it was decently trafficked. The combination of passing vehicles, along with the architectural fixtures in front of the home, like its several pillars and railings, could provide for some misleading and spooky-looking shadow play whenever headlights came down the street. Of course, this was all speculation on our part, and we'd put it to the test when we investigated the Glenn House once it was nighttime.

Leading Sounds

The first area we headed to was the kids' room, as the Glenn Family sadly lost three of their children at very young ages. If there was any emotionally charged paranormal activity occurring in the house, we speculated that it would most likely be tied to this room. We walked up the wooden stairwell to the expansive second floor and headed inside; we were greeted with an area fitted with antique furniture and peppered with children's toys throughout the room. Perhaps our minds have been trained by decades of horror films, but there's something unnerving about an old doll with lifeless eyes vacantly staring at you in the dead of night. It's always unsettling, especially when you're attempting to communicate with entities who may have passed away.

Since there were a multitude of reports associated with the Glenn House, we took a variegated approach to our equipment in the children's room. On this run we brought in a FLIR thermal imaging camera, ambisonic audio recorder, and Data Logger. We scanned the room, looking for any aberrant temperature hits on the toys. We restrained ourselves from speaking at first and hovered the camera through the darkness, peering at the screen and listening intently for any noises. We did this to become acclimated to the ambience of the home, to differentiate between outdoor noises and natural creaks and pops that occurred in the home.

But we also were intent to reach out to any entities there with the utmost respect. Again, multiple children died in this home and if we were going to try and speak to a grieving family member, or a small child, we wanted to do so with empathy.

> **Mustafa:** Throughout the course of our investigation at the Glenn House, Brandon and I kept remarking that we felt as if we had to tread lightly and there was a sense that we were encroaching on something private and that perhaps we shouldn't be there. It wasn't a negative feeling per se, but one where we felt like intruders, more so than some of the other cases we had investigated together in private homes.

We stood motionless in the night for some time before finally attempting to establish communication with anyone who was there.

We introduced ourselves, complimented the home, and asked if there were any members of the Glenn family present, keeping our eyes on both the FLIR screen and Data Logger. But there was nothing. We then began mentioning specific members of the Glenn family: Glenn, Sally, and eventually Sarah Glenn Marsh. Again we didn't document any activity. We were met with silence.

We then brought up David E., Henry, and Virgil, inviting them or any member of the Glenn family to play with the toys in front of us. We held our breaths, half expecting the figures or dolls to move in front of us. While that didn't happen, there was something that occurred out in the hallway that caught our attention. We looked at each other. There seemed to be movement in the hallway: the undeniable sound of footsteps.

After confirming no other members of our team were in the house during our investigation, we asked again if there were any children in the house. Again we were met with the same sounds in the hallway. We invited whoever was making the noises to come and join us in the children's room, but we were met with silence. We theorized that if there was indeed a paranormal entity making these noises, then they were either unwilling to come to the children's room, or they were attempting to draw our attention to another part of the house. So, staying on the second floor, we moved our equipment out of the children's room and into the hall itself, but stationed ourselves in the doorways of two separate side rooms across from one another.

We pursued our line of questioning, asking if there were any entities attempting to reach out to us and welcoming them to interact with our equipment. We waited for registers of environmental changes, again shifting our focus from the FLIR to the Data Logger while scanning the home to see where those noises would have possibly come from—a vent or draft from an open window—

but there was nothing. The noises in the hallway had stopped completely and it felt as dead and quiet as the children's room.

That is, until the quiet was punctuated by a loud noise that jolted us to attention. Our eyes immediately peered down the stairwell; it sounded like a door had slammed beneath us. We keyed our walkies to communicate with our team to ascertain if anyone had entered or left the house. But it was still just us and the cameraman; no one had been in or out. We sped down the stairwell to investigate the source of the sound. What's strange is that we could've sworn the loud noises we heard in the children's room were coming from the hallway, but now new noises were emanating from beneath our feet.

> **Mustafa:** After hearing the footsteps in the hallway and the door slam downstairs, and after it was verified no one from our crew made those noises, I knew Brandon was thinking the same thing as me: if this was paranormal, then we were being led somewhere by someone or something. What we wanted to try to ascertain, however, was why?

> **Brandon:** The phantom footsteps were an indication that we were on the verge of making direct contact with whoever may be haunting the Glenn House. My first instinct was to have everyone slow down and acknowledge that we were hearing the movement in the hall. As soon as we verbally acknowledged the footsteps, a disembodied voice followed shortly after. Upon review, the voice was a woman saying "bedroom." Interesting enough, later that evening we found one of the dresser drawers open in David Glenn's bedroom.

Without speaking to one another, we were both naturally drawn to the music room after arriving on the first floor. It was the epitome of bygone largesse with an antique piano standing in the corner, surrounded by other antiquities and period pieces. As we swept our FLIR camera through the time capsule, we placed our Data Logger on the piano bench. Before we could even step away from it and conduct a question-and-answer session, we heard a loud metallic noise of a jiggling door handle. Someone was trying to enter the room. We jumped back and looked where the sound was coming from: a door located next to the piano. A door, as the house was currently constructed, that led to nowhere. We braced ourselves and waited, expecting it to open, but the jiggling stopped as abruptly as it started.

It felt too perfectly timed, as if a member of the team was playing a prank. Because if they weren't, then we were dealing with an intelligent entity with a specific agenda we were still trying to wrap our heads around. We radioed our crew, but they were all stationed in the carriage house. To be sure no one had touched the door located near the piano, we conducted a thermal imaging scan of the door before interacting with it. There were no visible heat signatures or hand imprints. There was also no way that someone could have turned the handle from the other side, as that door was impossible to reach from the other side of the room.

Before jumping to any paranormal conclusions we asked ourselves: was there any way the handle could have moved on its own? When we tested the door and its handle, despite their age, we found they were both solidly constructed and couldn't find any reason as to why the knob would move or make noise unless someone had done so intentionally. Furthermore, after rotating the handle several times, we ascertained that the sound we made was identical to the one we'd heard (something we'd further solidify upon audio analysis during our evidence review). This wasn't the only strange occurrence involving doors in our investigation of the Glenn House, however.

Doors

Much like the children's room and hallway upstairs, the music room's investigation was at first punctuated with strange occurrences but was then followed by silence and a dearth of activity. As excited as we were at the prospect of speaking to an entity that potentially jiggled that door handle, slammed a door beneath us, or made footsteps in the hallway while we investigated the children's room, we couldn't document any concrete, on-command occurrences on our devices, or environmental changes. At least, not in the moment. It was frustrating to leave the music room without any in-the-moment evidence, especially in light of the activity we had just experienced.

We made our way out of the room to investigate the rest of the first floor. Directly across from the music room was the dining area, which carried some fairly significant claims. The most eerie was one experienced by a large group of people. While volunteers and visitors were conversing in the area during a tour, the walls reportedly shook, but the force seemed to originate from a central point in the room that quickly made its way throughout the area, as if there was an invisible tornado trapped in the walls that twirled around everyone.

> **Mustafa:** When I looked to natural causes for this type of phenomenon, I thought what they experienced was the result of an earthquake. While there are records of quakes occurring in Cape Girardeau, Missouri, there

weren't many. Furthermore, the dates we were given for this supposed paranormal occurrence didn't align with any of the earthquake dates in Cape Girardeau. Also, the tremors recorded in Cape Girardeau were all under the 2.5 magnitude mark, meaning they couldn't be physically felt by a human. The closest earthquakes of a greater magnitude occurred more than forty-nine miles away. While it's unlikely the phenomenon the volunteers and visitors experienced were the reverberations of an earthquake from a distance that far, I wanted to look at every possibility for the occurrence. Additionally, other factors like the water piping system in the home and the electrical wiring were all assessed by professionals. They were functioning as they should, so that was an unlikely reason for the strange event.

Brandon: We started to notice a change in the environment on our Data Logger while in the dining room. This was an indication that activity would soon follow. Pressure and temperature changes lead to yet another disembodied voice of a woman. Mustafa and I instantly played back the recording. The same voice that we experienced upstairs was collected on our audio recorder. This time she seemed to be screaming the word "no."

We carefully walked through the dining room and began inspecting our surroundings. Unlike the other areas we investigated, this room was punctuated with windows, allowing the blue glow of night to permeate our surroundings. We looked around, taking in the Glenn family's belongings, and commenting on how well preserved they were. Again, we began discussing the same aspects of the Glenn family history as we did in other rooms: David A. Glenn, the children they had lost in the home, their prominence in the community, and the unfortunate financial losses that lead to them losing the house. It wasn't until we discussed this insolvency that we heard noises that sounded like footsteps coming from the kitchen, similar to what we experienced in the children's room. We darted back to the kitchen area to try to ascertain the source of the noise, but we couldn't find any plausible explanation for what caused it in the moment.

We had run out of ideas. No matter where we were in the home, there was always some type of noise phenomenon just outside our immediate area that led us to another section of the home. So we regrouped in the dining room and tried to contextualize the nature of our findings thus far to piece together what was happening.

It seemed like the noises all pointed us to various doors and exits in the Glenn House, and we theorized that it was as if someone or something was trying to show us the way out. And while feelings are fickle and can change from moment to moment, the general sentiment that we had going into the building was that we weren't wanted in the Glenn House. That, coupled with all of the activity surrounding the various entryways in the home, led us to believe that we were possibly being accosted by an extremely possessive presence, which was understandable. The Glenn family were prominent members of Cape Girardeau society and their home was representative of all they had accomplished. They lost this home due to an unfortunate sequence of events that reversed their fortunes. If they were indeed back in their familial home, why would they want to leave or have outsiders inhabiting it and possibly reminding them of that loss? Were they threatened by the prospect of new owners taking over the home yet again?

That's when we decided to push the issue we believed was the most emotionally resonant with the location: the Glenn family's loss of the home they envisioned for themselves.

A Lost Home

Mustafa: Standing in the Glenn House's dining room, I made the decision to kick a paranormal hornet's nest, one that, in the moment, I felt was against my better judgment because my own family had lost our own home when I was younger.

I decided to challenge the Glenns' ownership of the home by stating it was no longer in their possession and if they were attempting to startle visitors into leaving the premises, they had no right to do so as it now technically belonged to Christy. I also discussed how Christy wanted to share the history of the home.

When I spoke to the Glenns not owning the home anymore, I happened to walk by a framed letter shared by Sarah Glenn Marsh, who had written how "love was built into the Glenn House from the ground up." I believe this to be 100 percent true; it was constructed to honor the union of David and Lula Glenn. It was near this letter I began to feel someone holding my arm. That grip then turned into an electric burning sensation that soon began to sting. I'd heard of people being scratched before, but never thought it would happen to me. When I showed my arm to Brandon, he immediately snapped a photo. Back in my hotel room later that night, when I got undressed for bed, I saw that the scratch was not only on my arm, but all down my back as well.

Brandon: As a paranormal investigator I always show respect to the entities. There are very few occasions when we will bring up a negative aspect of a location's history. Because there was so much mystery surrounding the activity at the Glenn House, Mustafa and I wanted to see if bringing up some of the more negative aspects of the Glenn family's history would lead us to more answers.

We wanted to replicate some of the talking points that were brought up in the historical tours of the home. When Mustafa told me that he felt a stinging sensation down his arm, we immediately looked at the affected area. Three scratch marks started to form in front of our eyes. It is significant that this happened while Mustafa stood in front of the letter written by Sarah Glenn Marsh. It is a coincidence that can't be ignored.

We had some guilt associated with taking this approach, as it was an emotionally charged subject. However, this investigative method did give us further evidence that there was a strong correlation between the Glenn family's ownership of the house and the supposed paranormal activity that had been occurring there.

Admittedly, it's impossible to know for certain what ultimately culminated in this scratch. All we could do is walk through our steps and logically analyze the data we had managed to gather up until that point. We listened to the recordings from our runs after the night's investigation had concluded. We could clearly hear the footsteps in the hallway, the door slam, the door handle jiggling, and the footsteps in the kitchen. We intently listened for any voices and reviewed our camera footage to see if anything occurred in the moments leading up to the scratch and well after it, but there was nothing.

All we had was a theory: that there were noises leading us to different parts of the home and for some reason one of the most significant pieces of evidence, which left a physical mark on a team member, had occurred in the dining room. But we still had other tests to run, and they involved descendants of the Glenn family: Sarah Glenn Marsh and her grandfather David Williams.

On the second night of investigating, we waited in the carriage house as Sarah and her grandfather made their way through the home on another tour of the premises. Since Christy said the paranormal activity ramped up considerably with each visit that Sarah made to the property, we wanted to see if her presence charged the building with more ghostly activity.

Revisiting the Dining Room

We began our follow-up night of investigations straight away in the dining room area, heading directly to the spot where the scratch occurred. We brought Data Loggers and motion detectors to see if anything was triggered should another physical event take place, along with a binaural microphone as we had recorded the sound anomalies from the previous night. It was then that we looked at the letter Sarah had written more in-depth. Since the scratch occurred near this letter, we wondered if the episode from the previous night had anything to do with the Glenn descendant's words about the home. We read the letter aloud, pausing in between each line, straining in the darkness to listen for any telltale footsteps or indication of an entity attempting to reach out.

Our eyes were peeled, fixated on the Data Logger. In between our pauses, we'd invite any entities to interact with the Data Logger, hopefully logging environmental changes, but there was nothing. However, we began to hear footsteps again, only this time they weren't in the kitchen or above our heads in the hallway outside of the children's room. This time the footsteps seemingly came from the main hall's entranceway just a few yards from us. That's when the familiar yellow glow from the Data Logger began to fill the room. Changes in barometric pressure began to register on the device, along with simultaneous temperature dips and spikes.

We were amazed. Were our constant exhortations to interact with our equipment finally being realized by the entities that may be there? It can take training for an entity to learn how to manipulate our devices, so theoretically someone or something could have elected to touch our device instead of our arms. We asked about the house again and if someone had tried to grab us the previous night. Nothing. We then asked if we had upset them by saying the home now belonged to Christy. That's when we were jolted by an audible screech or moan from a woman. The timing of the noise was uncanny and caused us to nearly jump into the antique ceiling.

Since our binaural microphone was recording, we went back to listen to the audio in real time, but it was difficult to ascertain what was being said, if anything. What we did know definitively in that moment, however, was that the screech sounded like an anguished person. Admittedly, the shout could be attributed to wildlife like otters in the area, but we found the sequence of events interesting. We asked pointed questions pertaining to the Glenn family in the area where the scratch occurred. Those questions were followed by footsteps, which were then followed by pressure changes, and then more questions, followed by the scream. It was intriguing, to say the least.

We persisted and repeated the same questions pertaining to the Glenn family, but any signs of activity in the area ultimately died down. We decided to reverse-trace our steps of the previous night's investigation to see if Sarah and David's visit might affect the activity in the upstairs portion of the home. We left the dining area and walked back upstairs to the hallway outside of the children's room, but as we did, we noticed that the front door was open.

This was the third time this occurred for us, not to mention the countless other occurrences with other team members. There was unexplained activity with doors in the home. As always, prior to investigating we ensured as close to a contained environment as possible; we knew that the front door was closed. We immediately recalled the footsteps we heard prior to the screech, but radioed our other team members to ensure no one had entered the house. Yet again we confirmed that no one had been in or out of the house during our investigation, thus ruling out the possibility a member of our crew was responsible for the door opening.

We stood by the door and tested its security as we had with the door in the music room the previous night. We ended up with the same result: there was no way that door was opening on its own. After closing the door and seeing it was, indeed, shut tight, we were about to proceed upstairs to commence the rest of our investigation. But right after we turned our backs, we were stopped in our tracks by movement near the front door and the sound of its handle jiggling. It then stopped as quickly as it started. Again there was no logical explanation for why this occurred. We stomped near the door to try to come up with a reason for the door handle moving on its own, and we opened and closed the door several times and waited for the noise to replicate itself. It never did.

Mustafa: Another interesting tidbit: Sarah informed me that when a producer from *Ghost Hunters* had contacted her to nail down filming dates for her to participate in our investigation, the power went out in her home. This happened despite there being clear skies and that never occurring in her home prior to, or after, that call. I thought this electrical aberration was interesting and believed there could be a possible connection to the Glenn House's own strange activity with the home's alarm system malfunctioning, despite there being no evidence there was anything wrong with it.

Brandon: Moments like this start to lead us down a path of a series of connections. The familial ties of Sarah Glenn Marsh and the Glenn family seem to be deeply connected. It is possible that Sarah Glenn Marsh is a catalyst for the activity in the Glenn House.

Prior to our arrival at the Glenn House, claims of doors opening by themselves were prevalent and Christy had even discussed this phenomenon during our tour of the premises. So what does it all mean? We kept noticing that whenever we tried to further investigate the home, something drew us to another section of the house. Twice on the second night our attention was guided toward the front door. Were any present entities in the Glenn House letting us know that we had overstayed our welcome and it was time for us to leave? Did they open the door to let us know it was time for us to go? Or were we allowing our historical understanding of the beautiful location and the Glenns' lineage to add fiction to perfectly rational occurrences that were coincidental? And why did the activity seemingly ramp up after Sarah and her grandfather visited?

Again, all we had were theories and sequences of events to go by, along with our own feelings throughout the investigation.

Our Conclusion

Mustafa: There's a temptation to attribute the activity in the Glenn House as inherently negative, especially when you consider the location's tragic past and my personal connection to the loss of a familial home.

However, when I met Sarah Glenn Marsh, there was an unmistakably positive outlook on life that she carried. She acknowledged the tragedies her recent ancestors endured, but her focus always magnified the better parts of their lives: the Glenns' charity, their work ethic, their love for family, and their ingenuity. Especially Sally, who appeared to have lived a remarkable life, even if her values may have been considered outside the norm for a woman of her time. Even though Sally had tragically taken her own life, she also saw great beauty in her life. Her passionate dreams of making it big in movies and the birth of David Williams, who eventually had children of his own, and then grandchildren. And one of those grandkids, through a confluence of seemingly unrelated events, came upon the home that no Glenn had been in for one hundred years. Life and time had indeed found a way to reunite the Glenns with the home they had cherished in Cape Girardeau.

Like any great investigation, we were left with throngs of questions following the activity we documented at the Glenn House. Did having Sarah in the home remind the

Glenns of their daughter that left home for the glamorous life of a would-be Hollywood starlet? Did that upset them? Or were they happy to have a living Glenn in the home again? Did that living connection bring them peace? And when that connection departed, did it percolate and boil over into inexplicable paranormal occurrences that baffled our team and those who sought to preserve the legacy of this historic location?

There's no way to put a convenient bow on this investigation, but to quote Nathaniel Hawthorne, the Glenns "had taken that downright plunge which, sooner or later, is the destiny of all families, whether princely or plebeian."[39] Or to put it more plainly as Leonardo DiCaprio's character in The Departed:[40] "Families are always rising and falling in America." For the Glenns, their rise and fall occurred in a matter of decades. Even though the ripples of that past tragedy are visible, after meeting Sarah Glenn Marsh and her grandfather David, it appears that the Glenn family name is on an upswing.

So what's in a name?

Well, if other members of the family are anything like Sarah, then I'd say there's a whole lot to the Glenns. Which is why I'm ambivalent about this case. I can only hope that I'm doing the same for my own family name, and I cherish this investigation because of it. It scares

39. Nathaniel Hawthorne, The House of the Seven Gables, 1851, Chapter 1, https://
www.cliffsnotes.com/literature/h/the-house-of-the-seven-gables/summary
-and-analysis/chapter-1/chapter-1-4.

40. The Departed, directed by Martin Scorsese (2006; New York: Warner Brothers,
2007), DVD.

me into thinking what could happen to my own life and forces me to cherish what I've accomplished.

Brandon: When we met with Christy for the reveal, it was pretty clear what type of haunting was taking place within the Glenn House. As we set up to show Christy the data that was collected, a tour was wrapping up and exiting the building. Just as the docent and tour walked over the threshold of the front door, the antique bell system started to ring. The same antique bell system that had its wires cut because it was frightening Christy on a weekly basis. I will never forget the look on Christy's face. What made this event even more significant is that the docent had informed Christy that this would be her last time giving a tour of the Glenn House.

It's almost as if the house was saying goodbye one last time. Taking everything into account, there is a strong familial tie with the Glenn family. I can't help but think about the immediate familiarity I had while walking into the Glenn House for the first time. This haunting was a mirror image of a case I had been investigating for a decade. A Victorian house that was more than a thousand miles away from the Glenn House.

In that other home, the McConaghy Estate in San Lorenzo, California, it was clear after many years of investigation, analysis, and unexplained data collected that these experiences typically happened when there was mention of the negative history associated with the family. This was an almost identical activity that was being experienced at the Glenn House. Two prominent Victorian families surrounded by tragedy.

From the photos of the disembodied dress captured by APRA investigator Bridget Odien at the McConaghy Estate, to all of the unexplained phenomena taking place in the downstairs study where one of the McConaghy family members passed away at the age of 101, the similarities of these two Victorian homes has led me to classify the Glenn House as a Class Two: Familial Haunting.

It seems that familial ties are just as strong in death as they are in life.

— 9 —
HOSPITAL PHENOMENA

Hospitals are commonly associated with birth, sickness, and death, so for many paranormal investigators, hospitals are of great interest for paranormal research and data collection. Since 2006 we have investigated many hospitals throughout the country. A common phenomenon has presented itself in a majority of these locations. In this chapter we will highlight one of the most haunted hospitals in the United States and how it falls within the classification system.

Possible Pseudo Haunting at
Galena Marine Hospital

- Galena, Illinois. Investigated in 2020 on A&E's *Ghost Hunters*. (Season two, episode six, "Haunted Hospital.")

Exterior of the Galena Marine Hospital.

Claims

- Moans and wails of pain.

- Footsteps in empty rooms, occurring "around" the individual.

- A voice yelling "get back to bed!" to a witness who spent the night.

- Echoes of a whooshing noise. One witness described it as a "tennis match."

- A puff of fog seen levitating in mid-air that eventually floats away from those who see it.

- A shadow of a floating torso seen with the naked eye.

- A shadow figure spotted on the stairwell leading to the top of the building toward the cupola.

- A sudden flash reported to randomly appear in the main level of the building. Interestingly enough, this figure allegedly occurs in accompaniment with the whooshing noise and also manifests in odd shapes, predominantly an "infinity symbol." The flash, like the fog, also purportedly floats on this main floor before disappearing.

- A witness claims they were "pulled" or "led" out of bed as if being gently woken up by someone.

- People have said they feel as if they are being watched both in and out of the building.

- While walking around the Galena Marine Hospital, several visitors have said they were touched by invisible hands.

- Random chills and cold spots are experienced throughout the building, even during the summer months. This is peculiar, given the building has no heating/cooling system, save for an old furnace in the basement.

- Witnesses have reported feeling suddenly ill while visiting the hospital. Upon exiting the building, they immediately feel fine.

History

We'd like to thank Galena local, historian/librarian Steve Repp, for his generous contributions to this section. Without his efforts, we wouldn't have gotten to become so acquainted with this historic town and his palpable enthusiasm for his work is a joy to be around.

Mustafa: As we parked our RV at the bottom of an embankment and trekked up a cold, muddy path in the woods, we could see bits of a formidable brick structure through the trees. When we breathlessly rounded up the earth toward the Galena Marine Hospital, it finally came into plain view. The first thought I had upon seeing the massive brick structure was, "What the hell is this doing here?" And as we investigated the hospital's history and conducted our paranormal research, we were left with more questions than answers. One fact kept nagging at me, however; this building was too stalwartly constructed in too strategic a location to be a mere coincidence.

Brandon: Upon arriving at the Galena Marine Hospital I was instantly taken aback by the placement of this beautiful building. Even after years of investigating abandoned hospitals, I was struck by the jarring nature of its presence among the trees; the structure appears as if it was dropped in the middle of the woods.

Great Earth

It can be argued that Galena is the most magical and ancient land in the world. As one of only two areas on our planet that were spared from the Ice Age's brutal geographical transmogrifications,[41] it may be the closest modern civilization gets to our planet's ancient past. Prior to this great arctic shift, Illinois was rife with substantial valleys that separated the earth, punctuated by treach-

---

41. Tony Briscoe, "The massive glacier that formed the Great Lakes is disappearing—and greenhouse gases are to blame for its untimely demise," *Chicago Tribune,* February 28, 2019, https://www.chicagotribune.com/news/ct-met-disappearing-glacier-great-lakes-20190213-story.html.

erous hills and redoubtable bluffs. However, the glacial freezes transformed Illinois and most of the Midwest, resulting in the uniform flatness that now characterizes the region. Galena retained its prehistoric beauty and differs visibly from its surrounding areas though, which became apparent the second we entered the small town.

The transmutations caused by the Ice Age also had a profound effect on the divergence of the Mississippi River, another key geographic fixture that played a crucial role in our nation's history. Glaciers diverted the body of water's path from east to west, and their eventual melting is responsible for the birth of the Illinois River.

This means that the very ground on which the hospital is built is a topographical wonder. Geological happenstance spared Galena from the Ice Age, rendering its land uniquely distinct from nearly every other part of the globe. The ancient rocks and minerals, which include granite, limestone, and lead, all remained untouched in Galena; the glacial floods only helped to usher in additional ore-rich sediment, surrounding the town with precious deposits. Even without Galena's storied past and historical implications, the area would still be a fascinating destination based on this uncanny fact alone.

A Native American General with a Thirst for Knowledge

The importance that Galena indirectly played in the Civil War cannot be overstated. Ulysses S. Grant not only hailed from this area, but so did eight other Union generals: John A. Rawlins, Jasper A. Maltby, John E. Smith, John C. Smith, John O. Duer, William R. Rowley, Augustus J. Chetlain, and Ely S. Parker. The latter general is one that's of particular importance to our investigation, as the man was handpicked by Grant to head the construction of the Galena Marine Hospital, but more on that later.

It could be said the reason Galena bred so many Union generals is that Ulysses S. Grant trusted these high-caliber men he personally knew to be of unshakeable determination. Given Grant's military record and resounding success in the Civil War, it's difficult to argue against his leadership, especially when it comes to his relationship with Ely S. Parker. Parker was the Tonawanda Seneca officer who was able to distinguish himself among his white peers, no small feat given the time period. Ely S. Parker may have had the single-most impressive ascension in the US military, especially considering his humble beginnings and the sociopolitical climate at the time. Born in 1828 in Indian Falls, New York, Ely went on to become not only a decorated soldier, but an attorney, engineer, and the first-ever Native American appointed as commissioner of Indian affairs, a distinction made by President Ulysses S. Grant himself.

Ely's birth name was Hasaonanda, but he had his name officially changed when he was baptized by his father, who worked as a miller and a minister. While Ely received a classic missionary school education, he was also brought up to embrace his Seneca heritage; he fluently spoke his native language as well as English. His parents urged him and his siblings to assiduously attend to their studies, and Ely's academic diligence culminated in a college career where he excelled tremendously.

His persistence landed him a position at a legal firm for three years in Ellicottville, New York, and although Ely applied to take the bar examination, he was not permitted to officially do so. Members of the Seneca tribe, like most Native Americans, were not considered US citizens. However, his deep knowledge of the law and job as a legal reader helped him cross paths with Lewis Henry Morgan, a fellow young lawyer who was fascinated with Native American tribes, particularly the Iroquois. The two collaborated on a book, *League of the Iroquois*, that faithfully represented the cultural practices of the Seneca and other Iroquois nation tribes.

It turns out this chance encounter would help shape not only the course of Ely Parker's life, but of America as well. Morgan dedicated the book to Ely and helped him secure enrollment at Rensselaer Polytechnic Institute in Troy, New York, to study engineering. Like most of Ely's academic pursuits, he created tremendous success through hard work; not long after completing his courses, he was able to secure employment as an engineer, a position he thrived in until the start of the Civil War.

A Seneca Diplomat and a Union General

Ely, not just content with his title as a civil engineer, also worked in public service functioning as an interpreter and diplomat to Seneca tribal chiefs. He primarily worked to aid them in US government negotiations pertaining to treaties and land rights. In 1852, Ely was named a sachem of the Seneca and nicknamed Donehogawa, which literally translates to "Keeper of the Western Door of the Long House of the Iroquois."[42] As it turned out, both of these vocations would prime Ely for an important role in the Civil War.

Ely's body of work as an engineer includes a litany of important structural contributions, chief among them important upgrades and maintenance projects to the Erie Canal. He was also made supervisor of all government projects in Galena, Illinois. Again,

---

42. Dee Brown, *Bury My Heart at Wounded Knee*, 1970.

this was no small task for a Native American from New York who recently graduated from engineering school.

Ulysses S. Grant, after moving to Galena from St. Louis in 1860, developed a strong friendship with Ely, and was instrumental in allowing the Senecan to serve in the Civil War. After enlistments opened, Ely attempted to put together a regiment of Iroquois volunteers to fight for the Union army; however, New York governor Edwin D. Morgan rebuffed the idea. Undeterred in his mission to serve, Ely then tried to enlist as an engineer in the hopes that his specialization would supersede the military's stringent ban against Native Americans joining the service. However, he was again denied entry in the Union army, this time by Secretary of War Simon Cameron. Ely persisted, this time enlisting the help of his friend Ulysses S. Grant, inquiring if any of his units needed engineers. It just so happened they did.

Ely officially became a member of the Union army and was sent to report under General John Eugene Smith, where he was appointed chief engineer of the 7th Division during the Siege of Vicksburg. Distinguishing himself during the siege, Ely then joined Grant as his adjutant during the Union army's Chattanooga Campaign and the two were transferred to the US army headquarters. It was here the two worked together throughout the Overland Campaign, and at the Siege of Petersburg, Ely was given the title of Grant's military secretary. All of Grant's written correspondence was handled by Ely, which includes the surrender documents that were drafted and ultimately signed by Robert E. Lee.

Ely was present at the historic Appomattox Court House meeting of Union and Confederate generals, which ultimately saw the end of the war. He often told his family and friends about the historic day, specifically the moment when General Lee "stared at

[him] for a moment ... extended his hand and said, 'I am glad to see one real American here.' "[43] To which Ely reportedly responded, "I shook his hand and said, 'We are all Americans.' "

Ely's pivotal role in the Civil War assisting with the construction of siege technology and tactics, along with drafting important documents and continually being a trusted source to Ulysses S. Grant, earned him a great deal of esteem. Consequently, he was brevetted brigadier general of United States Volunteers on April 9, 1865. Less than two years later, he was promoted to brigadier general of the US Army on March 2, 1867. Following the Civil War, his service distinctions continued, as did his work as a liaison between the United States government and Native American tribes throughout the country, with a heavy focus on negotiating with southeastern tribes that allied themselves with the Confederacy during the war.

A History of Lead and Bullets

Galena's proximity to the Mississippi River, along with its abundant lead deposits, were responsible for its inception as a town in 1800s. However, as early as the 1600s the area was often frequented by the Fox and Sac Indians who mined for lead, which they initially used for a variety of purposes. Prior to the French's discovery of the area, Natives would typically grind lead down to use for decorative purposes like warpaint or in burial ceremonies. They were also known to be extremely secretive about the location of their lead mines, understanding the mineral's significance.

When explorers charting the New World arrived from France in the 1700s, the Fox (Meskwaki) Native Americans would trade

---

43. "Ely Parker: Iroquois Chief and Union Officer," HistoryNet, 2021, https:// www.historynet.com/ely-parker-iroquois-chief-and-union-officer.htm.

lead ore for French goods, including guns and knives. The French would then smelt the lead ore and turn it into bullets. For providing the raw materials to produce them, Natives would then receive some of the ammunition these visitors created, along with lessons on how to craft lead into other items such as cooking utensils, statues, tools, and net sinkers.

The area's closeness to the Mississippi River, combined with its lead mining activities, helped establish it as an important trade outpost, and as the years progressed, Galena officially became a town in 1826. Although its name was derived from the scientific term for lead-sulfide, Galena soon became a major trading destination where a variety of goods and services were offered. Steamboats and other shipping vessels were constantly passing through the town and there was such an abundance of wealth that Galena was soon bigger than Chicago. Galena boasted a population of fifteen thousand people in the 1850s, which was absolutely massive for its time.

All of the commerce and travel to and through Galena also meant there were more individuals at any given time in need of basic human services, chief among them healthcare. It's no secret that life on the water, especially on a steamboat, was arduous and lonely. This was one of the main reasons cited in newspapers at the time for the construction of the Galena Marine Hospital.

On Valentine's Day in 1854, a resolution in the House of Representatives was first proposed by Congressman Washburne, who argued that boat laborers and the large influx of people passing through Galena needed a hospital dedicated to their needs. Proposals for the building were first officially opened on December 16, 1856, some six months after President Abraham Lincoln first visited Galena, Illinois, in the town's famously upscale DeSoto House, which still stands today. (We ate there; it's a fantastic location.) A copy of the official advertisement can be found in a January 3, 1857, issue of *The Washington Union* newspaper asking for contractors to erect the building "according to plans and specifications prepared at this department."[44] Ely was tasked with designing the Galena Marine Hospital for "roustabouts," aka in this case, unskilled deckhands.

The Hospital's Many Lives

Ely S. Parker was already involved with a number of local projects in Galena, and he was commissioned to plan and oversee the Galena Marine Hospital's construction. Some two years after it was built, however, the Civil War broke out, which severely inhibited traffic on the Mississippi River. Galena was no exception. While it's believed the hospital was converted to adapt to the needs of soldiers, there aren't many records that indicate this is necessarily the case. It's not out of the realm of possibility to think that soldiers were cared for in the Galena Marine Hospital, but it seems that its primary purpose was to provide a medical haven for the denizens who traveled up and down the Mississippi to pursue commercial interests, which nearly came to a standstill during the four years of Northern/Southern conflict in the United States.

Since vessels weren't traveling farther south for trade, the need for the hospital waned. It officially closed its doors in 1865, and in 1868 was purchased and transformed into the Northwest German English Normal School. But this didn't last long, and the school moved to a different location around 1890.

For the latter part of the century leading up to the first quarter of the 1900s, the hospital remained all but empty. There are

---

44. *The Washington Union*, January 3, 1857, newspapers.com.

advertisements that date back to 1926 that refer to the area as the Nash Sanitarium. While the moniker holds medical connotations, it was primarily billed as a rest stop for commuters who traveled farther than ever before thanks to the advent of the automobile. The hospital itself wasn't inhabited until 1912 by the Nash Medical Company that did business there for approximately twenty-one years before moving out. The hospital stayed vacant for years. Then during the 1950s, there were plans to turn the building into an apartment complex, but that idea never came to fruition. The hospital has remained empty ever since. Private owners have purchased and sold the structure several times, but never for any specific purpose. It appears that folks typically buy the Galena Marine Hospital for the large amount of land it sits on and due to the fact the building is so stalwart and holds such a prominent place in Galena's history.

The Marine Hospital's Patients

An 1854 newspaper article delineated the hospital's purpose in very plain terms:

> "Many of the seamen have no homes ... You see somebody must take care of those men when they get sick. There is no place for them on the boats, and the diseases are often infectious. Then if they were to be put off at any landing the inhabitants would grumble, and in reality no county or town should be compelled to keep men who are not residents."[45]

Seamen often stayed at the hospital during this time, not only to receive treatment for their ailments, but in many instances

---

45. "Hospital for Roustabouts," Newspapers.com, 1854.

merely to have a place to stay on dry land and find refuge from the elements. These sailors, even if looked down upon by this particular newspaper reporter, were a vital component of Galena's economy, as goods traveling up and down the Mississippi helped further cement the town's identity as an important trading post.

These goods were primarily trafficked on steamboats, and these vessels (as our guest investigator and local naval expert, a steamboat captain himself, told us), were "living organisms" on their own. Operating a steamboat requires a tremendous amount of finesse and careful commandeering. Even the most experienced captains could find themselves in danger. Something that Captain Daniel Smith Harris of the *Grey Eagle* discovered on May 9, 1861,[46] when the $65,000 vessel (more than $2 million today, adjusted for inflation) wrecked at Rock Island Railroad Bridge.

Despite it being his only boating accident in an immaculate thirty-two years as a captain, Daniel Smith Harris quit being a seaman at fifty-three years of age. His name was redoubtable among sailors and fellow captains, which was why the utter destruction of the *Grey Eagle* came as such a surprise. An article about the event published in a local newspaper states: "One of the most shocking marine accidents took place about five o'clock yesterday afternoon when the sidewheel steamer *Grey Eagle*, Capt. D. Smith Harris commanding on her down trip in passing the bridge struck the pier of the Illinois side of the draw. It stuck forward of her wheel house, stove the boat and sank her to her brass almost instantly."[47] The

---

46. "Steamer Grey Eagle Is Wrecked," Iowa History Project, May 9, 1861, http://iagenweb.org/history/rivers/greyeaglewreck.htm.

47. "Steamer Grey Eagle Is Wrecked," Iowa History Project, May 9, 1861, http://iagenweb.org/history/rivers/greyeaglewreck.htm.

wreckage occurred less than a month after the Civil War had officially gone underway.

It's also worth mentioning that seamen of this time period were
thought to be a tight-knit group of people, as life on boats was usually hard, isolating, and ever-changing, especially on a steamboat.
Those who worked the rivers became well acquainted with one
another; deckhands made themselves familiar with the different
vessels and the captains who headed them. Not only would they
have known of Daniel Smith Harris's stellar record, but would have
also shared and gossiped over the absolute shock that he had sunk
a $2 million vessel at such a seemingly innocuous portion of his
journey downriver. It's tantamount to being an expert *Super Mario
Bros.* player and dying by the first goomba in stage one, or dropping
a pop fly ball during the World Series after being named league
MVP ten seasons in a row.

It was this community of sailors who initially inhabited the
Galena Marine Hospital, along with the doctors and medical personnel who staffed the building. And while there's a temptation to
immediately attribute the paranormal claims to these aforementioned individuals, we must keep in mind that the location has seen
many lives and purposes throughout its time, so the entity or entities could be from any time period. Are there Civil-War-era sailors
still lingering among the structure's cold bricks? Or are there spirits
of students striving for a higher education at the heart of these
hauntings? Perhaps it was an employee of the Nash Medical Company, or maybe a different type of entity that saw the abandoned
building and decided to turn it into its home.

Then there was the curious location of the Marine Hospital: it
was built in the heart of a munitions oasis and commissioned the

same year as the *Grey Eagle* and President Lincoln's historic visit to the town.

> **Mustafa:** What interests me most about the construction of the Galena Marine Hospital is its timeline. The idea/plans for the hospital's erection were first formulated in 1856, some four years before Ulysses S. Grant and Ely S. Parker reportedly met. To me, the strategic positioning of the Galena Marine Hospital as a military vantage point right before the Civil War seemed too coincidental. I'd be lying if I didn't say I hoped our investigation provided answers to these questions and greater insight into this location's mysterious placement in the middle of the woods.

> **Brandon:** Anytime we talk about the formula of a haunting, history plays a huge part in that process. History is the foundation of our research. Without looking deep into a location's history, we would never truly understand the workings of a haunted place. Certain historical events play a role into the unexplained phenomena at a location like the Galena Marine Hospital. It is absolutely crucial that we look at all avenues of a building's history prior to our investigation.

The Living

- Frank Budreck, owner/groundskeeper of the Galena Marine Hospital at the time of our investigation, who experienced several paranormal occurrences.

The Dead

- Weary sailors and seamen who sought refuge and comfort within the walls of the hospital.

- Ely S. Parker and/or other notable individuals who helped build the hospital who may be able to speak to the mystery surrounding this location.

- Captain Daniel Smith Harris or those who worked with him, or any other notable figures from Galena who frequented the hospital.

- Possible inhuman entities that are reportedly known to shack up in hospitals.

Investigation

While we had tons of questions regarding the conspicuous placement of the hospital, we had to put them aside and direct our attention to our client. The building's current owner was in desperate need of answers and was looking for two things. Firstly, an affirmation or practical explanation of the paranormal activity he and other witnesses believed they encountered on several occasions. While on our tour of the premises, he claims to have seen, with his own eyes, a "mysterious fog" that came "out of nowhere." After this strange mist caught his attention, it hovered for a few seconds before ultimately, as he says, "running away."

We also learned there were several instances of perceived visual phenomena of a disembodied, half-torso shadow figure floating through the halls of the hospital. While it sounds like something straight out of *Ghostbusters* or *Pac-Man* game, it calls into question the type of entities that may or may not be haunting the hospital.

The idea of inhuman entities is one we usually refrain from addressing or discussing on the program, as the majority of paranormal claims are either easily explained, or, if there is any spooky activity going on, they seem to communicate in familiar, human ways. However, as we've learned in other hospital investigations, like our case in Pampa, Texas, that we discuss later in the book, sometimes we're faced with situations that suggest we're communicating with a being that has a darker or more aggressive feel. Would we come across an entity like this in Galena?

Some of the other claims we felt could easily be explained right off the bat: the moans and wails of individuals can almost always be attributed to local wildlife. Since the Galena Marine Hospital certainly saw its fair share of tragic accidents, including some unsavory boat disasters, explosions, and all sorts of injuries, it's easy to misconstrue a noise an animal makes as a human in pain. Which is especially understandable when a person spends a considerable amount of time secluded in an old building in the woods that has such a deep history.

This could also account for the sensation of being watched. The "invisible hands" that people felt while ambling the halls of the Galena Marine Hospital could directly be attributed to drafts in the old structure. We were tempted to attribute possible drafts to the random "cold spots" that witnesses claimed to experience in the building, but as we found out, these occurred during the more sweltering summer months, and there wasn't any form of air conditioning in the building. Just an old heater/furnace that really only kept the basement warm.

The footsteps, too, could be directly addressed to the general age of the hospital, or so we thought. Wood is a living, breathing material of sorts, and it's not difficult to imagine someone would start to hear a snap, crackle, or pop on a stairwell above them and mistake it for a person's footstep.

The second question Frank had was a tall order: were the denizens that frequented this lonely sailor's haven a stone's throw from the Mississippi in the middle of the forest still here? And if so, what did they want? That was a question we couldn't promise to answer, mostly because all of the prep work, research, and investigating in the world can't guarantee a definitive answer, which is something a lot of our clients have a difficult time wrapping their heads around. Thankfully Frank was gracious enough to temper his expectation to solve a mystery in our week-long stay there, but his concern for these sailors was legitimate.

Traditional ghost stories almost always depict entities as tormented beings that haunt a location due to some past trauma. It's impossible to know whether or not this is the case or that even addressing this trauma is the most fruitful way of conducting an investigation. Think about it: if you were meeting someone for the first time, would you want a total stranger probing into your personal business and bringing up the most painful memories of your past?

> **Mustafa:** Personally, if someone asked me that, I'd tell them to go kick rocks.

Understandably, the building's owner was concerned that if he was indeed experiencing a legitimate paranormal phenomenon, that it was somehow tied to some unsavory fates that seamen suffered prior to being admitted to the hospital. Steamboats were notoriously prone to grisly accidents, and Galena has seen its fair share of naval tragedies. So Frank wanted to know: was he an unwilling spectator to the agonizing moments in someone's life that they were forever trapped to relive? Was the pain far too great for these spirits to relinquish?

It's an unenviable position to be put in when you're asked to exorcise entities that are theoretically languishing for all eternity. It's important to note again that these are all suppositions introduced into our collective consciousness from centuries of supernatural storytelling.

Whether from religious traditions, gothic literature, or popular TV shows and movies, we cannot allow ourselves to take on the role of savior for ghosts that are presumably persecuted by the negative happenings of their corporeal existence. As paranormal investigators, our goal was to attempt to practically replicate the paranormal claims our client and witnesses reportedly experienced. If we were able to document them and subject them to further scientific scrutiny, then all the better.

> **Mustafa:** Brandon said something about the Galena Marine Hospital's placement that sticks with me to this very day: the history will unlock the mystery of this location. And while I don't feel like I have a solid grip on exactly what the hospital's history is, I do know it provided a refuge of sorts for me, like it did for the many roustabouts that traveled up and down the Mississippi so long ago. While life on the road away from my family wasn't easy, I felt more at home in the Galena Marine Hospital than I did at my lovely hotel in the area (the place had a friggin' waterslide and a lovely free breakfast for crying out loud). I'm also not blind to the fact that there are folks who raise an eyebrow

at the work Brandon and I do. I have people outright scoff when I tell them I'm a paranormal investigator. But there's something to be said about going to great lengths to not only seriously document the supposed strange activity in a place like Galena, but vying to do your best work possible, even if you aren't respected by large denizens of society. And while I have it infinitely easier than the sailors, deckhands, and various laborers who toiled on these steamboats, I hoped I could connect with them, at the very least by appreciating the mere presence of this hospital. The circumstances that culminated in my team's being there were vastly different than the ones that brought travelers to Galena some 150 years ago, but I'd like to think that there were other folks who were relieved to be there too.

It's that respect for my work that I bring into the investigation that I hoped would resonate with any spirits or remnants of people that still lingered in the hospital.

Brandon: When I told Mustafa that history will unlock the mystery of this location, I was sticking with the proven formula for our investigations. It is very easy to be overwhelmed by a building like the Galena Marine Hospital. As a paranormal investigator you have to keep reminding yourself that historical fact, factual data, and empirical evidence will give you the answers you need at the end of the day.

Cold Earth

Traversing the outer grounds of the Galena Marine Hospital was one of our first orders of business, primarily because outdoor investigations are some of the most difficult to conduct. Capturing viable audio is almost impossible due to external contamination, namely in this case the wind and loud trudging of our footsteps through the snow. We recorded anyway, but the circumstances were less than ideal. Then there was the fact that during our investigation, Galena experienced record below-zero temperatures every day, so the sooner in the night we tackled the claims surrounding the hospital, the less freezing we'd be.

Because we were layered so thick with clothing, experiencing any of the physical claims like being touched by unseen hands would be significant. We decided to bring a FLIR thermal imaging camera in an attempt to document any heat imprints should they turn up on our clothing, which would be extremely interesting considering the gelidity. But even more important was the potential of spotting any visual anomalies in the frigid air. Unsurprisingly, all of our surroundings registered as cold on the FLIR, so if there was an entity traversing the grounds outside of the Galena Marine Hospital, we'd theoretically be able to see it on our FLIR thermal imaging camera in real time.

As we trudged through the snow, keeping our eyes peeled and ears open, we weren't able to register any anomalous events during our initial canvassing of the area surrounding the hospital. There were no aberrant heat signatures, no experiences of the claims that folks had while visiting the site, and nothing that seemed out of the ordinary when we surveyed the cupola and looked through the windows of the hospital. We were on the lookout for the strange infinity symbol light anomaly that reportedly manifested itself on the main floor of the building, but again, there was nothing from our investigation outside, looking into the hospital, that would suggest strange occurrences were happening indoors. But we had strategically placed several devices inside the building as we conducted our investigation outdoors, chief among them an Electron Multiplying Camera and a Data Logger.

Blue Lights

Unbeknownst to us as we walked the cold grounds outside the hospital, we were able to document yet another event that highlighted a recurring theme: the strange light phenomena we constantly witnessed in varying forms across multiple investigations. And we came face to face with it yet again.

After learning from Frank of this running light and fog on the main floor, we placed our EMCCD camera, along with a standard 4K lockoff camera, both facing a Data Logger that would record any environmental changes. These were recording throughout the entire investigation and thankfully this placement would provide us with real-time correlating evidence of photonic activity.

Mustafa: While Daryl and I were warming ourselves by a barrel fire our team built outside to keep us toasty between runs, we discussed the different claims in the building. That's when I saw Daryl perk his head up toward the main floor. His pupils were fully dilated and he began exclaiming he'd seen a light. I followed his gaze and I too saw a glowing blue light appear before quickly dissipating from the windows. I shot a look to my wide-eyed cameraman who lifted his camera to record as he followed Daryl and me into the building. We wanted to witness the anomaly firsthand, but when we reached the main floor, it was gone as quickly as it had manifested. I held my breath as I ran to the EMCCD camera, hoping it was still recording.

It had been running the entire time, hell yes. I breathed a sigh of relief and immediately stopped the recording, fetched the SD card, and brought the footage to the rest of the team.

Brandon: When Mustafa brought me the SD card from the EMCCD camera to review on the spot, I knew the experiment I had set up provided results. Hours before Mustafa and Daryl's experience, I'd set up a Data Logger in the direct line of sight of the EMCCD camera to see if we could document any environmental changes when photon events started to manifest. Moments before the blue light started to appear out of nowhere, pressure changes were recorded on the Data Logger. Just as the changes ceased, the room was engulfed in a strange blue light. This was the first time we recorded environmental changes in conjunction with documented photon events.

The photon event that illuminated the entire main floor of the Galena Marine Hospital was witnessed by nearly every member of the *Ghost Hunters* cast and crew. But for our purposes, secondhand accounts and anecdotes just wouldn't cut it. We needed documentation of its existence. Playing back video of the event in real time was one of the most exhilarating moments of our careers. Once we saw the footage, we were blown away by what we captured.

The anomaly begins with what can only be described as a shimmer of blue light populating the screen in nonconsecutive pillars; it almost looked like a snowstorm of blue static. This shimmer was punctuated by individual photon events bleeding into the image, manifesting apparently out of nowhere. The cold blue storm then starts to completely dissipate as the other photon events also die down. What was most interesting to us was that we could see the Data Logger at the end of the room register distinct changes in barometric pressure as these uncanny events occurred. Prior to the photon event, there were no fluctuations of pressure occurring in the room. The device only registered these changes when the illumination manifested itself, establishing, yet again, a distinct correlation between these fantastic photon events and pressure changes.

These are the kind of advancements that paranormal investigators dream of, and we were living it right then and there.

> **Mustafa:** It's always emotional when I can find evidence of a witness's paranormal claims they swore they experienced in a specific location. For years I worried that my brother, my mother, and I had some shared temporary bout of insanity when we saw all of the cabinets and drawers in my childhood home open and close by themselves that one life-altering evening. So it's personally vindicating when we can undoubtedly capture a phenomenon that's haunted someone so much they feel compelled to call others for help. For us to provide that relief in any way we can is not something I take for

granted. I will admit though, this particular case may leave Frank with more questions than answers. But he can rest assured that he's not crazy; there are strange light anomalies happening on the main floor of the Galena Marine Hospital and we've got the footage to prove it.

Brandon: Every time we investigate a location, our goal is to deliver the truth. Moments like our breakthrough at the Galena Marine Hospital are what keeps me going in this field. It's one thing to go to a location expecting to find something. It's a whole new experience when you can walk away with factual data to back up a person's claims. Moving forward from this investigation, we now know that barometric pressure and photon events have something to do with the phenomenon taking place at locations throughout the world.

Going Further

We ascertained that there were some significantly spooky things occurring at the Galena Marine Hospital that we were luckily able to capture on camera and corroborate on multiple devices. However, we weren't able to establish a conversational back-and-forth with an entity that may be there, which is a great way to ascertain whether or not the haunting is being caused by an intelligent force. That's what we had hoped to establish moving forward in our case in the hospital.

Several runs with multiple team members in the basement yielded little more than a few pressure changes on a stairwell. The problem was these environmental alterations were not only short-lived, but they also didn't seem to correlate with any of our lines of questioning. We decided to head farther up the hospital, closer to the source of the strange light we had documented. Our time was limited on the premises and we wanted to follow the strongest leads we had. A glowing blue light that manifested out of nowhere seemed impetus enough to focus our efforts there.

> **Mustafa:** Since that blue light was captured while Daryl and I were outdoors, we wanted to replicate the environmental conditions that lead to this strange phenomenon. We split our teams into two; I investigated indoors with Daryl while Brandon and another member of the team canvassed the grounds outside, FLIR thermal imaging camera in tow.

We had already documented strange activity, but now we wanted to try to get to the bottom of it, or at the very least, replicate and capture it again. We started on the first floor of the building, right beneath the room where the EMCCD camera and Data Logger were placed and where we captured the blue light. We placed a motion detector between two Data Loggers, along with an ambisonic microphone, in the area of the room where some of the visual anomalies were reported. Our thought process was that we could potentially chart the movement of an entity's trajectory by monitoring the sequence in which the devices were activated. We initially attempted to establish a line of communication with any entities that may be there by casting a wide net of questioning, welcoming anyone or anything present to interact with us. Calling our investigation quiet would be an understatement. Our devices hadn't registered any changes, save for some drops in temperature on our Data Loggers, which was natural given the increasingly cold atmosphere of our location. Our motion detector hadn't been triggered, nor did we hear any sounds in the building that seemed out of the ordinary.

No pun intended, but at this point the Galena Marine Hospital was dead.

We introduced ourselves and called out to any potential entities that may be present on the premises, inviting them to interact with our devices to alert them of our presence. We waited in silence. Nothing happened.

We demonstrated the various ways they could interact with our devices, showing how movements and actions would set off our devices. We also welcomed any entities who wanted to speak with us to go up to the ambisonic microphone and tell us whatever they wanted so we could listen to the recording at a later time.

Still. Nothing. So we decided to talk amongst ourselves about the Marine Hospital's history. As is sometimes the case in investigations, discussing various talking points about a location and not trying to pointedly communicate with someone or something can result in activity. However, this indirect communication fell flat. We were just two ghost enthusiasts sitting in a spooky building, freezing our butts off.

The Captain

While we always follow strict investigative protocols steeped in empiricism when we work, the emotional component of our cases cannot be denied. Again, since the entities we deal with are presumably human, it makes sense to attempt to connect with them on a human level. Which is why we enlisted the help of a local cap-tain, a man who not only has a deep-rooted affinity for steamboats, but also piloted them his entire life. It was his childhood fascination with these particular vessels that influenced and defined his entire career path.

Our discussions with the captain not only further convinced us for his love for naval transportation, but Galena's history and the livelihood of sailors who oft traversed the waters of the Mis-sissippi. He enthusiastically shared his knowledge of the town's naval history and the prominent captains who steered their vessels in and out of it. We can say this without hyperbole: there proba-bly wasn't any living individual who could potentially connect with the Galena Marine Hospital's earliest denizens more effectively than the captain. What's more is that we were the first paranormal investigative team he had ever encountered, and he was gracious enough to aid us in our case and function as a sort of trigger per-son. We wanted to see if there would be a change in activity after introducing him into the hospital.

> **Mustafa:** I'm always amazed whenever we encounter something in real time that could be paranormal in nature. There are many investigative moments left out of TV: the hours of work that are conducted in com-plete silence and the litany of thoroughly researched facts and tidbits we invoke that yield no results whatso-ever. In many cases, our work is more akin to a stakeout than anything.
>
> So I felt incredibly spoiled after the first leg of our investigation at the Galena Marine Hospital. To not only secure evidence of a photon event in the same area

our client witnessed it, but to corroborate that phenomenon with pressure changes elated me immensely. And while I was happy to be the captain's paranormal first and appreciated the fact I got to work with someone else who assiduously pursued their childhood dream, I certainly wasn't expecting that his presence would have as significant an impact on our investigation as it did.

I can't overstate this. The captain completely altered the course of our work in Galena, helping us document some truly remarkable findings that were corroborated both inside the hospital and outside where Brandon was with the FLIR thermal imaging camera.

Brandon: Utilizing trigger objects can really pay off in certain situations within a paranormal investigation. This was the first investigation that I was part of that used a living person as a trigger object. As I've stated many times, history plays a huge role in the formula of a haunting. Bringing in a living, breathing captain that knows about this particular location's history is the perfect way to try to trigger activity. It definitely paid off.

After bringing the captain in, we explained how a typical investigation works. Then we attempted to address the entities there again with him present, but were still met with dead air. There was only one thing left to try: have the captain directly address any of the ghosts that may or may not be present. So we encouraged him to do so, but he seemed a bit reluctant at first. "What do I say?" he asked us. We told him to just speak to the entities directly and ask any question he wanted an answer to, anything at all.

One question from the captain was all it took to shift our case in an entirely new direction. He asked if anyone present was familiar with Daniel Smith Harris, the naval legend who retired after sinking the *Grey Eagle*. When he did, the activity ramped up immediately.

Not only did we start receiving pressure hits on our Data Logger, but the motion detector was triggered, and we began to hear footsteps above us in the stairwell leading to the cupola. They weren't the familiar sounds of the building settling. They were loud, distinct footsteps: *bum, bum, bum*. Heavy, deliberate. Shocked and ecstatic, we asked our guest to keep speaking to the history of the location, and he inquired about the conditions of the sailors present and asked if anyone personally knew Harris. Again, we heard more footsteps and noises from above us and our Data Logger continued to register pressure changes with another instance of the motion detector being set off. Before we could fully wrap our heads around what was happening, after only a few seconds transpired after the activity spiked, our walkie sounded indoors.

> **Mustafa:** Brandon's call to Daryl and me indoors was right on cue; it occurred a mere moment after the captain conducted his first-ever investigation. My theory is that because his ties to the location are so genuine and the entities recognized a fellow naval man, they were more willing to speak with him than any one of us. It's hard to blame them. The most time I spent on boats up until that point were ones I could paddle with my feet or the promo yacht we rode for the premiere of the show. I was just happy to witness such an amazing sequence of events kicked off by our guest investigator.

Brandon: One of the main claims outside of the hospital was the sensation of being watched. Being that there was a lookout tower on top of the structure, I wanted to scan the tower with the thermal imaging camera. I knew that if any activity was taking place while Mustafa and Daryl were conducting their experiment, it could also be taking place in the tower above them.

What we captured outdoors on the FLIR appeared to corroborate with what was happening simultaneously indoors: accompanying the noises leading up to the cupola was a clear image of a man. His heat signature was a jarring anomaly in the thermal camera's cold surroundings and he appeared to be standing and peering off into the distance. We confirmed there were no living people upstairs and, in a matter of seconds, the strange outline of a person vanished.

The order in which all of this phenomenon occurred is truly staggering and we believe the sequence of events strongly suggests its impetus was the captain. Not only did we register environmental changes with several devices in a short duration of time, but they occurred in accordance with the mentions of Captain Daniel Smith Harris and his naval career.

When the activity on the first floor halted, our team raced up the stairs in an attempt to potentially document other paranormal occurrences. But, like the onset of the night's investigative work, we were met with silence. Our adrenaline was still pumping, however, as it was hard to shake the high of the captain's input sparking yet another strange sequence of events for our team to wrap our heads around.

Further Investigation Required

While these finds were especially fascinating to us paranormal geeks and they opened up exciting new investigation possibilities to pursue to push our research forward, what did they ultimately mean to Frank? Were there any spirits of sailors in anguish? Were souls tortured by the grisly steamboat accidents reliving their darkest moments, pining away in misery at the Galena Marine Hospital?

It's impossible to know what plane of existence these supposed entities were residing in and any attempt to reconcile or explain that would be pure conjecture on our part. Culture has influenced our understanding of life after death. From religion, to Hollywood, to oral traditions, to stories, to wishful thinking, to propaganda, humanity has worked tirelessly to try and give meaning to our lives on this planet. In doing so, we've created a slew of ghostly narratives that influence how we perceive paranormal activity and the unexplained.

Here's what we do know: there is something strange going on at the Galena Marine Hospital. We were able to document many of the claims that witnesses experienced in the location and further expound on them by corroborating simultaneous, measurable phenomenon as they occurred. That activity ramped up when we introduced an individual with a deep emotional connection to the building and the traveling sailors it was built for. Sailors who persisted, by all accounts, through difficult lives. Sailors who found solace in the building's presence. Perhaps someone who could truly commiserate with their struggles is what coaxed them into reaching out to our team. If they were just looking for relief from their torment, one would think they'd latch on to whoever would listen. But it could be that acknowledgment from a person these entities could identify with is what they desired most. A fellow brother-in-arms if you will, who wouldn't judge, but could appreciate what they endured. Someone they'd feel at ease sharing their stories and drinks with in front of a fire to pass the time until they were back on the water, feeding the living, breathing steamboats carrying them to their next destination.

> **Mustafa:** I don't know if we'll ever get to the bottom of why the Marine Hospital was constructed in the first place. Or if there is a relationship between the work Ely S. Parker did for the United States government and the building's conspicuous placement among the well-mined lead deposits that gave Native tribes, along with French settlers and merchants, their livelihoods. Mines that ultimately gave birth to Galena and handed the town its namesake. However, like so many people who traveled to this land untouched by Mother Nature's harshest brutalities, our team discovered wonders that would transcend our work to unimaginable new heights. And for that I'm thankful, even if I am still left with questions that'll probably never be answered in my lifetime. I was given something better: a clear direction to even more exciting prospects that will further this field into new horizons, a field I've dedicated my life to and one that is vastly misunderstood.

Other Instances of Photon Events

This wouldn't be the first or last time we'd hear claims of clouds or hazy films in our paranormal investigations with *Ghost Hunters*. Residents of the boarding house in Clifton, Arizona, (season two, episodes one and two, "Terror Town") had multiple claims of an uncanny mist that traveled between two rooms. We were able to utilize the EMCCD camera to capture inexplicable visual photon events spiraling in atypical patterns in the exact location this phenomenon reportedly occurred. The EMCCD again proved vital in supplanting further fog claims in our investigation at the Halsingland Hotel in Haines, Alaska, (season two, episode five, "Alone in Alaska"). What's interesting about the cloud in Haines was that we were not only able to document it with the EMCCD camera, but we further supported the theory that it was paranormal in nature after capturing other aberrations in the same area with our body cam, ambisonic microphone, and Data Logger on two separate occasions.

The case of the Galena Marine Hospital, unbeknownst to us at the top of our investigation, would only further establish one of the most important scientific breakthroughs in the paranormal field. While we had already collected two profoundly significant instances of photon events tied to longstanding paranormal claims, this case would not only defy our expectations, but leave us with a litany of new questions that presented exciting possibilities. The most intriguing aspect was that multiple devices not only corroborated these claims, but there's evidence that suggests this phenomenon was deeply intertwined with the maritime history of the hospital, thanks to our guest investigator.

Our Conclusion

Brandon: As with many cases within this field, the Galena Marine Hospital remains a mystery. One thing I do know is that we made a tremendous breakthrough in documenting environmental changes simultaneously with photon events. Hospital phenomena has always been something that is of great interest to my research. Now that we have further information behind the possible mechanics of manifestation, we will have to look for further patterns in locations like the Galena Marine Hospital. Because of the lack of historical context, we classify the haunting of this seemingly active former hospital as a Class Five: Pseudo Haunting.

— 10 —
A NURSE'S CRY FOR HELP

The following account of a haunted hospital reminds us of the tragic humanity of some hauntings.

Guilt Ridden Entity / Suicide Apparition Haunting at Worley Hospital

- Pampa, Texas. Investigated in 2019 on A&E's *Ghost Hunters*. (Season one, episode twelve, "Hospital Horror.")

Claims

- Shadow figures appearing in windows.
- One of the owners spotted a figure dressed in black walking through the halls.
- Feelings of dread.

- Sense of danger; individuals who had no knowledge of the paranormal claims felt as if something was telling them to get out of the building.

History

A big thank you goes out to the city of Pampa, along with *Ghost Hunters* producer, Kaylen Hadley, who worked tirelessly on this case and provided further notes and background for this and other sections.

> **Mustafa:** Our intuition isn't always right. In fact, many times when we simply follow our feelings in a given situation, it only results in more confusion or leads us down paths we wish we could retrace. But it's at Worley Hospital where I learned that sometimes not ignoring that intuition could unlock the answers to everything we seek. Built out of what was once a dire need in a town filled with opportunities long gone, the Worley Hospital is where I learned to not cast away or dismiss something I thought I saw. It taught me to follow through on it, come what may. By taking that leap of faith, I was able to not only form a deeper connection with a true friend, but also an unseen resident with a tragic past who I think is filled with regret for succumbing to a permanent solution to a temporary problem. A resident who was haunted herself by the choices she made and a loss of love.

Brandon: After years of investigating locations across the county, I thought I had experienced my share of complex cases. The old Worley Hospital changed everything I thought I knew about hospital phenomena. This was one of the most convincing instances of communicating with an energy that retained consciousness.

There are parts of Pampa that certainly fit the bill of a ghost town. The main street is barren and peppered with long-closed storefronts that once shilled goods that are long obsolete. Traversing these wide roads punctuated by mostly empty buildings on foot at night made us feel like we were in the tense, nighttime shootout scene of *No Country for Old Men*, except we were on the lookout for ghosts, not a guy with a terrible bob haircut holding a cattle gun. The bar is the exact opposite of an Instagrammable spot that sells $9 craft IPAs and deep-fried pickles with made-in-house mustard. Pampa's not a superficially trendy place by any means, but that didn't matter to us. It provided the perfect setting for our investigation, and we were welcomed with open arms by many of its residents.

And while at first glance it'd be easy to classify Pampa as another dry, American flatland county that bleeds into another one, like a gaping amalgamation of Walmarts, Chili's, and chain retailers, Pampa has its own feel. The Coney Island Cafe serves up fare that can only be described as classic Americana and is objectively delicious. The *Pampa News* headquarters still publishes printed newspapers and proudly retains its journalistic integrity while respecting its history. And a short walk from this building that houses massive, made-to-last printing presses and all of the town's deeper secrets stands the equally formidable Worley Hospital.

A Tale of Two Accidents

Located in the heart of town on West Francis Avenue, the hospital was named after its founder, Phebe Allan Jackson Worley.[48] She was married to Henry, the first sheriff of Clay County, and the two owned and lived on the ranch they built between Wildorado and Hereford. It was on this land they thrived and had three children: S. Burt, Inez, and Amanda. When Henry wasn't maintaining law and order in the county, he was tending to his ranch. One tragic day while herding cattle, Henry was thrown from his horse and died. Since he had ridden days away from his family, the cowboys under his employ buried him near Wichita Falls in Charlie, Texas, and it took them eleven days before they returned to the ranch, cattle in tow, but no Henry. This is when Phebe learned of her husband's fatal accident, and the ranch fell into her hands. She mourned him by persisting and began to oversee all ranch operations along with the property's foreman, Albert Combs. The ranch thrived under Phebe's guidance; the Worleys were financially stable but had no idea the luck they would strike after tragically losing Henry so young.

Phebe laid the foundation for her family's success before Pampa was even Pampa; it was first named Glasgow, then Sutton, before ultimately being named after the Pampas grasslands of South America. Phebe managed to carve out a viable living for herself and her family well before Pampa saw its leg of the Sante Fe Railway built in 1888, a development that brought monumental changes to the region over the course of eighteen years. This only helped her

---

48. Eloise Lane, "The Legacy of Phebe Worley," White Deer Land Museum, excerpt from the story of Earnest and Amanda Reynolds in Gray County Heritage FOCUS, Summer 1992, p. 13, https://pampamuseum.org/phebe -worley/.

already stalwart work ethic bring in greater profits, and then in 1916 oil was discovered in the Texas Panhandle. Pampa enjoyed a significant largesse of the energy source brimming under its earth. The financial boom was so great the Gray County seat of government was officially moved from Lefors to Pampa, where it still stands today.

The nature of Pampa's economy had drastically changed since the discovery of this oil. Property became a hot commodity and, with harsh winters shifting ranch hands' business prospects considerably, livestock trade and dairy farming were no longer Phebe and other landowners' primary sources of income. Men who knew how to drill for oil hit up ranches all over the Panhandle, and it was only a matter of time before they approached Phebe. After settling on a lease agreement and contract, these men, hungry for liquid gold, got to drilling. In 1925, on a day the Worley family would probably never forget, Phebe and her children rejoiced. It was confirmed there was indeed oil lurking beneath their land. Their lease agreement earned them considerable profits and their lives were forever changed as a result of the discovery.

It was this confluence of events, and probably the tragic accident of her dear Henry decades prior, that ultimately influenced Phebe to build Pampa's second hospital. After becoming injured in a car accident herself, the ranch hand and modest oil tycoon decided enough was enough. She commissioned Worley Hospital's construction under the firm belief that one hospital in the area wasn't enough, especially with the influx of laborers and newfound business ventures that completely transformed Phebe's hometown into a world she never imagined. With assistance from a local doctor, Phebe secured financing to build the massive structure on West Francis Avenue, and it served the population of Pampa until well after the oil boom was over. She didn't want any other person in the area to undergo what she and Henry endured by being too far away from potentially lifesaving care.

However, Pampa's boom, like all unprecedented flare-ups, didn't last forever. After the businessmen left when the land dried up, the town's economy stagnated. Soon Worley Hospital's existence was difficult to justify with Pampa Regional Medical Center (established in 1950) caring for a greater number of patients and generally handling the needs of the town's dwindling population (which, at the time of our investigation, was 17,068). This ultimately forced Worley Hospital to close its doors in the mid-seventies.[49] Newspaper articles wrote of its impending cease of operations, praising Phebe as a benefactress and for having the foresight to ensure that all of its citizens and growing workforce had greater healthcare options in the region.

Although Phebe Worley died only six years after her hospital was commissioned, its legacy lived on. We'd experience this legacy firsthand after tirelessly working to uncover the mystery behind Worley Hospital's supposed hauntings more than forty years after it was abandoned, a shell of the necessary haven she envisioned it would become. A hospital built out of Phebe's haunted past when she received the news as a young woman that her husband was dead, and the rest was now up to her.

A Nurse's Cry for Help

Brandon: When investigating a former hospital, you enter an uphill battle trying to figure out who you might be communicating with. This was definitely the case with the old Worley Hospital... until night two. Musta-

---

49. "Worley Hospital Faces Closure, Opened in 1928," *Pampa Daily News*, September 5, 1975.

fa's brilliant research, coupled with following our protocols, gave us some of the most interesting results I have
ever encountered.

Mustafa: Even though we're on a show called *Ghost
Hunters*, our work extends far beyond simply encoun-
tering/experiencing paranormal entities. What we do
is investigative in nature, which means I always find
myself feeling like a detective. If you've ever attended a
group paranormal event, you've probably encountered
these overzealous Columbos who whip out their K2
meters and immediately start addressing the victims or
transgressors in urban legends, hoping to crack the case
of a decades-long mystery that probably didn't occur in
the first place.

Even when one has the facts of the case on their
side, it's important to keep sound investigative protocols
in place and not jump the gun on if what you experience
is paranormal or not, but also if the entity you've established contact with is indeed the person you assume it is.

In the 130+ investigations I've partaken in, I've never
come across a single case where I was entirely sure I
knew who I was speaking to. Except for one: Worley
Hospital. Have I captured strange EVPs? Absolutely.
Have I managed to document full-body apparitions after
speaking about a particular person associated with a
building? Yes. But I was never certain whom I was speaking to.

At Worley Hospital, I am extremely confident we not only established contact with an unseen entity, but know exactly whom we spoke to.

And it all begins with a nurse named Mary.

Mary Lucille Stayton was a Dayton, Texas, native who enlisted in the military in 1942 as a nurse and was promoted to lieutenant shortly after. In the few surviving photographs of the young woman, she's sporting ebullient smiles; she appears to be with a patient in one, beaming from ear to ear while working at the Great Lakes Naval Training Center. The other shows her standing in a group of UNS nurses, all in uniform and posing before a United States Naval Hospital, presumably a graduation of some kind.

Her sparse records card indicates that after fulfilling her duties at Great Lakes, she reported to Norfolk, Virginia, then Kingsville, Texas, before heading to Oakland, California. It's in the Golden State where she likely met the man who'd later become her husband, Alfred Myers.

Alfred joined the military two years before Mary, and while the little evidence we have of Mary's service shows her relishing her work and having a great experience, Alfred's time wasn't as kind to him.

His mother feared he had been severely injured or killed in action when she stopped receiving letters from him after a nearly two-year absence. Then in late September of 1943, she received a message that Alfred was "all fine" and "in good health." The message was sent from a Japanese POW camp where Alfred was held prisoner. While documentation pertaining to the treatment he endured is sparse, the treatment American POWs suffered during World War II is the stuff of horror films.[50] It's not a stretch to assume that Myers was subjected to severe abuse, torture, and psychological trauma during his time as a prisoner. Alfred was stationed at Fort Mills (Corregidor) in the Philippines, which came under Japanese control in May of 1942. He was ultimately liberated from the camp at the end of the war, along with sixty-one other US servicemen on September 5, 1945. They were escorted on a naval vessel off the coast of Osaka, thus ending his nearly three-and-a-half-year nightmare as a prisoner of war.

Most military personnel traveling from Japan recuperated in California, so it's safe to assume this is where Alfred and Mary first met as she was stationed there at the time. This theory is further supported by the fact Mary officially filed her resignation less than a week before Thanksgiving in 1945. The reason for her resignation: marriage. She was granted passage home on December 6, 1945, and headed to Pampa, where Alfred resided for seven years before enlisting. Mary had a job waiting for her at Worley Hospital as a surgical nurse and she started shortly after leaving California and the military for good. Her official records card indicates Mary's honorable discharge was processed on March 6, 1946; her name was changed to Mary Lucille Myers.

Nineteen days later, she'd be dead.

A March 26, 1946, *Pampa News* article told the story of a twenty-five-year-old nurse who attempted to ingest cyanide twice in the same day while on shift at Worley Hospital. "She was reportedly despondent over domestic affairs," the news clipping reads. Doctors said she had intentionally locked herself in a room early in the

---

50. Kirk Spitzer / Yokkaichi, "The American POWs Still Waiting for an Apology From Japan 70 Years Later," *TIME*, September 12, 2014, https://time.com /3334677/pow-world-war-two-usa-japan/.

evening on March 25 so she could poison herself without interference. The physicians were able to stave off her passing until two in the morning, but no longer. Mary Lucille Myers had succeeded in taking her life.

After her death, Alfred went on to marry another woman from Pampa and the two had six children together.

While Mary met a tragic end, we believe her story was far from over.

The Living

- The owners (two cousins) who purchased Worley Hospital in hopes of turning it into a bed-and-breakfast.

- Contractors hired for the job who were too frightened to work there; the spooky stories impeded work on the building from ever happening.

The Dead

- Phebe Worley, the matriarch of Worley Hospital.

- Any number of patients who were treated at Worley Hospital, some of them violent offenders.

- Mary Lucille Myers, a nurse who tragically took her own life while at the hospital.

Investigation

Condemned. It's a loaded word with two very different meanings that are tragically appropriate for our investigation at Worley Hospital. The punishing heat made our daytime walk-through of the premises quite the ordeal. It didn't help that there were throngs of dead pigeons whose limbs, brutally torn apart by intruding cats, decorated the building's hallways and crannies, either. On its exterior, Worley Hospital was a boarded-up rectangle with shards of cracked wood covering windows, some smashed, some dirty but intact, as well as long-unused doorways covered in dust and bird excrement. The walls inside were decorated with graffiti. If one ambled alone through Worley's halls at night with nothing but a flashlight, they'd certainly feel they were in a horror film.

This would especially be the case if one were privy to some of the more violent injuries the town and hospital had seen. Healthcare centers are no strangers to death, a topic that paranormal investigators are always quick to attach to when working a case. In theory, one would think *where* someone died matters much less than *how* they met their demise. Some of our fondest and most heartrending memories are tied more to circumstance and feeling rather than physical surroundings, after all. So before investigating the undeniably creepy hospital, we reminded ourselves not to initially invest too much mental energy in the vicious shovel murder of Homer D. McIlvain at the hands of James Ogleby. It was a fight between the two that culminated in Homer reportedly slashing James across the throat, which prompted James to grab a shovel and strike him with it. Both men's wounds were treated. Homer died; James didn't.

There was also the accident of E.E. McKee, an employee of the local Pampa packing plant, who had his arm nearly torn off in a car accident. It was so badly mangled that doctors couldn't save it. Worley has surely seen its fair share of death and tragedy, however, like any hospital, it was also the source of relief and joyous moments for throngs of people. Children were born there, people were healed of their ailments, and lives were saved.

The two cousins who purchased the hospital weren't intimidated by Worley's history or the formidable task of renovating the building into a bed-and-breakfast. They purchased it in 2019, excited to embark on the daunting project, but soon noticed strange activity that almost always culminated in feelings of unease or inexplicable bouts of fear.

They weren't the only ones who experienced such activity. Friends and hired contractors refused to spend extended periods of time in the building, which meant the two were effectively condemned themselves, their dreams for Worley halted. They called us to get to the bottom of their experiences to see if their minds were playing tricks on them. And if there was indeed paranormal activity occurring within the walls of Worley, what then?

The most significant claims were the feelings of dread those who frequented the hospital endured. Practically speaking, that was a tall order to rule out as there were no infrasound or EMF to speak of to influence temporal lobe activity.

> **Mustafa:** I was skeptical about attributing the feelings of dread to anything paranormal from the second I stepped foot inside Worley Hospital. If I owned it, I'd lease the place to Halloween horror house planners and probably turn a pretty profit based on its ambience and spray-painted walls alone. You can't discount how much of an effect your mind plays in a haunting. I could see myself easily getting psyched out walking the building's hallways and taking in the satanic imagery, pentagrams, rudimentary devil-men drawings, and creepy messages vandals plastered on the walls over the many years it's been closed.
>
> After researching some of the more unsavory stories associated with both Pampa and the hospital, I saw how folks obsessed with the macabre and supernatural

might find themselves latching onto easily debunked occurrences as evidence of paranormal activity. In 1932, John Clugey was admitted into the hospital after being shot three times after a drunken fight. Phebe Worley, the amazing founder of the hospital, had died there from natural causes and even had a room dedicated to her. Then there's the sordid tale of Homer and James, along with E.L. Emerson who was crushed between a truck and a trailer and died while undergoing a blood transfusion. There was also the tragic case of Raymond Lee, a baby who died only two and a half hours after being born.

The one story I couldn't shake was that of Mary Lucille Myers, which I elected to ignore and not bring up much in the course of our investigation. But that didn't mean Mary's story ignored us. Still, as in every case, I kept an open mind.

Brandon: Anytime a client reports experiencing feelings of dread, we have to look at the obvious natural explanations. One thing we noticed right away were the train tracks not far from the building. It's possible the passing trains could cause infrasound in the abandoned hospital. Is there a source of high EMF making them feel a sense of dread? On our first investigative run of the building, Mustafa and I not only tested the building for infrasound as a train passed, but we also conducted an EMF sweep of the entire hospital. We were unable to document the proper hertz and decibel ranges that cause temporal lobe activity. Being that the building didn't have electricity or running water, we were not able to find any man-made EMF sources. We had to look at possible paranormal causes for these reported feelings of dread.

Shadows and Sounds

While touring the first floor of Worley during the day, we were able to speak with local paranormal investigator Tonya Trimble. Tonya relayed to us a strange encounter she and her team had during the course of a first-floor investigation. While in a side room at the far end of the hallway, they heard noises as if something was being dragged across the floor. As they attempted to ascertain where the sound came from, they walked out of a room they had entered and saw a chair smack dab in the middle of the hallway, a chair that wasn't there before. She also reported she and her team glimpsed a shadow figure darting passed them at one point but couldn't document any evidence of its existence. And throughout their case work they noted a sensation of being watched.

We kept this in mind when nightfall arrived and we were tasked with investigating the first floor. We performed another EMF sweep, reconfirming there weren't any electromagnetic frequencies present in the building. This was unsurprising, given the fact that all internal wiring in Worley Hospital had been effectively dead for decades. It'd be highly unlikely that any of these spooky feelings could be influenced by EMF. Although Worley was especially quiet at night, with even less exterior road traffic and/or the chatter of birds and other creatures to consider, we still wanted to test the location's infrasound level. Our OmniMic feedback, however, yielded little to no ultralow frequencies from either internal or external sources that could be the cause for said feelings of dread.

It was safe to assume the feelings of dread experienced by the building's owners, Tonya Trimble, contractors who worked on the premises, and others who've spent time in Worley were caused by virtue of walking through a decrepit building with scary imagery graffitied on the walls, or there was truly some inexplicable activity going on.

In addition to our Data Logger and OmniMic, we implemented the use of other devices for our investigation: an ambisonic microphone and strategically placed lockoff cameras throughout the building's hallways. While there weren't any notable audio claims associated with Worley Hospital, we wanted to have an enhanced audio recording running in case an object was dragged across the floor like Tonya claimed to have heard. We placed lockoff cameras in the main hallway in the hopes we'd capture any of the shadow figures witnesses claimed to have seen. And lastly, due to the size of the building and the claims that these figures usually appeared unexpectedly or in people's peripheral vision, we equipped ourselves with body cameras in case such a phenomenon occurred. We then walked from room to dilapidated room on the first floor with our Data Logger, attempting to reach out to any entities that may be present while instructing them to interact with our devices.

At first, the investigation was quiet. We didn't register any significant changes on our Data Logger, save for the odd drop in temperature, which was normal given the changes in temperature as the night carried on. We did experience, however, the sensation of being watched—it certainly *felt* like we were not alone.

These were only feelings without any evidence or documentation, so we largely ignored them and continued with our investigation, methodically heading into different rooms and areas until we eventually ended up in a room at the end of the hall. We placed our Data Logger on the floor and began to conduct a question-and-answer session. We kept our questions broad without immediately jumping to any specific names of individuals associated with Pampa or Worley Hospital and opened the floor to any entities that may be present.

It wasn't long before we heard noises coming from one of the rooms.

The sounds of shuffling feet emerged from an area down the hall, followed by pressure changes on our Data Logger. We immediately made the connection to Tonya's experiences—here we were in a room at the end of the hall, just like she was, and suddenly we heard strange noises coming from another part of the floor.

We tried establishing communication with the entity that may have been there. We referenced the noise we heard, as well as the chair Tonya said had moved, but our Data Logger yielded no further environmental changes. We ventured out of the room at the far west section of the first floor and proceeded to the spot where we'd heard noises. There was a chair smack dab in the middle of it. Were we in the midst of another chair-moving phenomenon? We addressed the noise again, inviting any entities present to interact with our Data Logger. Nothing. That's when we had an idea: let's move the chair into the hallway where Tonya saw it during the course of her investigation to see if that drummed up any activity. This hallway also happened to be in view of the lockoff camera.

We set the chair in the middle of the hallway and waited to see if it stirred up any activity. We asked questions again, giving time between each one. Then we asked if they were all right with us moving the chair. The same shuffling noise occurred, but this time at the other end of the hallway, closer to where we were when we'd first heard noises in the *middle* of the hallway. Why were the sounds always out of reach? Were we being sent to different parts of the hallway for a reason?

What was remarkable about this instance, however, is there appeared to be a visual anomaly associated with the noise: a shadow had walked from one room to the other. We quickly confirmed with the rest of the team and crew that no one had traversed the grounds outside of the building and that no cars had driven past the front of Worley; everyone had been stationary. So what caused the shadow?

There was a good chance it could be an animal, even if the shadow did appear tall. We wanted to rule out the possibility of a cat or other creature coming into the building, as there were remains of pigeons splattered all over the floor. But our FLIR thermal imaging scans yielded no imprints or signs of an animal crossing the floor in the building, dispelling our thought that there was possibly something skulking about as we investigated. As we looked through the rooms trying to ascertain a practical explanation for what just happened, our investigation took a dramatic turn.

Mustafa: At this moment, Brandon shouted to me that he saw a figure peek out at him in the middle of the hallway, before retreating behind a wall leading to the stairwell going up to the second floor. Thankfully the body cam on his hip was directed straight at it. I must have asked him, "Did you get it? Please tell me we got it!" at least a dozen times.

Brandon: As I stood in the middle of the hallway, I sensed I was being watched. Just as I turned around, I witnessed a three-foot-tall figure peeking out from one of the pillars. This was the exact area that our clients sensed the

feelings of dread and witnessed a shadow figure. Being
that I was wearing a body camera, I knew I must have
captured what I saw. This would be the first time we collected compelling visual evidence on a body cam.

We tried to establish lines of communication multiple times
with the entity we thought we saw on the first floor, imploring
them to interact with our Data Logger or speak into our ambisonic
microphone. We asked if they were a patient in the hospital. If
they were an employee at the hospital. We talked of Phebe Worley and some of the accidents that occurred there. We spoke of
its place in Pampa and if they were upset that it closed down, or
happy that it opened. We asked if they were a resident of Pampa
or if they were from out of town. But all of our questions had the
same response: nothing.

With our run officially cold and plenty of footage to analyze,
we were excited to get right into evidence review, especially of the
footage captured in the middle of the hallway during that intense
moment when we were sure we spotted a visual anomaly.

The body camera footage we obtained during our first-floor
run-through of Worley is a baffling find. There is clearly shadow
movement captured on the body camera, and our attempts to
re-create it proved fruitless. What's more is that the lockoff camera didn't pick up the visual anomaly. This led us to two possible
conclusions: the first being that even though we couldn't re-create
the anomaly no matter how often we tried, that it was somehow a
glitch or aberrance caused by the angle of our camera placement
at the end of the hall. The second being that the frame rate of the
body camera, for whatever reason, was more adept at picking up
apparitions and documenting their presence. This second possible
conclusion is made even more interesting following our astound-

ing find at the Halsingland Hotel in Haines, Alaska (*Ghost Hunters*, season two, episode five, "Alone in Alaska"), which clearly displays a similar figure peering out into the hallway, once, twice, and then disappearing behind a wall.

Instinct

Building off our most significant find from our first night of investigating, we decided to expand on this line of thinking. We packed virtually the same equipment with the addition of two motion detectors. If there was an entity or animal moving throughout the halls, then these devices should be able to document their presence. What differentiated this run from our previous one was that every member of the *Ghost Hunters* team was present in the building, with two members downstairs performing demolition work. The theory was that new construction, or at the least a substantial racket, would incite some paranormal activity.

We set up our devices in the hallway directly above the area where we had previously spotted the shadow figure. Our ambisonic recorder was running, picking up each sledgehammer strike beneath us. Our motion detectors, despite the vibration and racket, weren't set off. In fact, we thought they were malfunctioning and even stepped in front of them to ensure they were functioning properly—they were. No environmental changes were being registered on our Data Logger either. Between the punctuated silence from the ruckus occurring beneath us, we decided to walk up and down the halls of Worley's second floor to see if we could verify what we had seen previously instead of waiting for an entity to approach our devices.

And we did.

Mustafa: At least, I thought I did. I got a feeling, call it intuition or instinct, but something told me to look to my left. I second-guessed myself the entire time and tried to dismiss my hunch that told me to go into that room. It's at this point I told myself "screw it" and decided to open my mouth instead of trying to rationalize what I thought I saw. I told Brandon I swore I saw something in the room to the left of me. We walked in and my hair immediately stood on end—we weren't alone. I felt cold and the Data Logger I held registered EMF spikes. There was something setting the device off, and neither Brandon or I had any idea who or what it could be.

Brandon: Anytime we conduct EMF sweeps, we have to be very cautions of these readings. Does it mean we're documenting evidence of ghosts? It's unlikely. But when Mustafa followed his intuition and walked into that room, something out of the ordinary took place. I believe the EMF spikes and Mustafa's reaction had something to do with the activity manifesting at Worley Hospital.

The EMF hits were the first anyone on our team experienced throughout our entire investigation at Worley Hospital. We attempted to see if any of our devices—cell phones, walkies, cameras—set off the Data Logger. Nothing. We asked if there was anyone here with us and the EMF spiked again. We waited, and asked again, if there was anyone here with us, and if there was, if they could set the device off like we believe they just did.

The device registered another EMF hit. We thanked the entity we were theoretically speaking with and asked if we were talking with someone who worked in the hospital.

Another hit.

In exciting situations like this, it's important to ask control questions to narrow down the possibility of who you think you're speaking with and to look for any practical explanation as to what could be setting off your device. This is why checking for rhythms or patterns is vital. If the device goes off on its own in measured increments, there's probably some electrical interference or device glitch causing it to occur.

However, we were getting what appeared to be direct responses to our line of questioning, so we decided to implement control queries to further ascertain who we were speaking with.

We asked if we were speaking to someone who was a patient in the hospital. Nothing. Then we asked again if we were talking with someone who worked in the hospital. Yet another EMF spike.

We asked if we were speaking with a doctor in the hospital. Nothing. We asked if we were speaking with someone who worked as a custodian or janitor in the hospital. Nothing.

Mustafa: It's at this moment that Brandon and I looked at each other and had a strong feeling we knew exactly who we were speaking to. We just couldn't believe our theory was beginning to take shape before our very eyes. While researching the history of Worley Hospital, the tragic tale of Mary Lucille Myers stood out to us above all else. We both agreed that if there was someone haunting the location, it made the most sense that Mary would be the person still there. While Phebe Worley was the matriarch of the hospital, Mary's ties were undeniable. Not only was the hospital where she ended her life, but it could be a place that was an escape from her troublesome home situation. Additionally, the personal sacrifices a woman of her time had to make to become a nurse were not insignificant. The entirety of her adult life was dedicated to excelling at a vocation she, by all accounts, cherished and thrived in. So for her to take her own life while on duty in a building that was her haven led us to believe there was a strong possibility she could still be tied to this location.

But even we couldn't predict just how much evidence we'd collect to support our theory.

Brandon: It is a rare occurrence to verify that you are speaking with a certain entity. That rare occurrence was taking place before our eyes at Worley Hospital. This moment was a huge breakthrough for our work with the classification system. Everything that I had been working on since 2006 came into play in this interaction. Our quest to connect history with science was happening in front of us.

When we asked if the person we were speaking to worked there as a nurse, a surgical nurse specifically, our Data Logger instantly registered an EMF spike. As a control, we questioned if we were speaking to a doctor, saying we were just trying to be sure. There was no EMF spike. When we asked again if we were talking to a nurse, we documented yet another EMF spike.

To further narrow down our Q&A, we asked if we were speaking to a man. Nothing. We asked if we were speaking to a woman; there was another EMF spike. Then we asked if we were speaking to Mary Lucille Myers and we were met with several EMF spikes. We waited before asking once more if we were speaking with Mary Lucille Myers and again our device registered EMF hits.

After picking up our jaws off the floor, we radioed our other team members, alerting them to what we believed was an intelligent entity that had quickly learned to manipulate our equipment in order to communicate with us. We asked what type of activity they had encountered upstairs. Aside from some odd noises, they hadn't experienced anything out of the ordinary.

After relaying our findings from the second floor, they suggested we send the entity upstairs to them, and ask if the entity could set off their Data Logger. It hadn't been registering any significant environmental changes or EMF throughout the demolition derby going on downstairs over the course of our investigation directly beneath them. They were stationed in the surgery room upstairs, so we asked the entity to visit our three team members and interact with their Data Logger as they had with ours, clearly delineating it was the same device as the one we held.

Less than a minute later, our other team members began registering EMF changes on their device. They asked similar questions, throwing in control queries as we had, which yielded the same results as us. It was remarkable.

Motion

Mustafa: It's difficult to condense a week-long investigation into a forty-three-minute episode of television, but it was especially tough for our case at Worley. Brandon and I had experienced nearly a half hour of direct communication across various devices, and other team members got in on the interactions as well. Before we even reviewed our evidence, we knew we were dealing with one of the most significant paranormal finds we'd ever come across.

Brandon: Prior to our analysis, Mustafa and I knew that we were dealing with something very significant. Putting a protocol in place was really paying off. It was only a matter of time before we could draw a conclusion as to what class of haunting was manifesting at Worley.

Our team members then asked the entity to return to the second floor to continue the conversation with us. What followed threw us for a loop: one of our motion detectors turned on. We looked around the room for evidence of a shadow figure, and then to the Data Logger to see if it was registering EMF spikes. It wasn't. The pale blue light of the motion detector then began to fade. So we asked if we were speaking with Mary again, and asked her to set off the device as she had done previously. While the Data Logger remained flat, the blue light of the motion detector turned on. And it stayed on.

Here's how this motion detector works: if someone stands in front of it, its light will stay on. When you back away or move to the side of the device, or you stand completely still, then the light begins to fade and completely turns off, until it registers movement again.

Since the light had stayed on for well over a minute, we wondered if it could be that Mary, or whatever entity was there, elected to utilize the motion detector to communicate with us instead of the Data Logger. And if that was the case, what was the reason? We assumed the motion detector was malfunctioning, but continued to actively communicate with Mary. We asked that if she was indeed standing in front of it, could she step back and only turn the light on to answer "yes" to our questions?

In a matter of seconds, the light dimmed before completely going dark. We looked at one another in amazement before asking Mary to reconfirm she was there by stepping in front of the motion detector. Right on cue, the light was set off.

What proceeded next was a series of yes and no questions pertaining to Mary, filled with more control questions. We seemed to corroborate time and again that there was a person there named Mary Lucille Myers who worked as a surgical nurse. We inquired about the demolition work and if it had disturbed her (it did, according to the light going on again) and if she was familiar with the new owners (she was). We were reluctant to delve into the topic of her suicide attempt. We put off any line of questioning pertaining to it by first attempting to discuss the possibility of her coexisting peacefully with whoever entered the building, be it Worley Hospital's new owners or a slew of new guests who would potentially stay there in the future.

When we asked if it would please her to see the hospital renovated and its rooms filled with visitors, she appeared to answer in the affirmative by setting off the blue light of the motion detector. We confirmed this using control questions and varying the frequency of our queries: "Would it make you happy to see these halls filled with people again? Turn that light on as you have—" Before we could finish the sentence, the motion detector turned on. After it died down, we asked one more time, "Would that make you happy?" Again blue light filled the room.

Our back-and-forth lasted longer than any communication session we'd ever participated in before (or since). It continued until we exhausted all questions pertaining to the client's fears and corroborated to the best of our ability given the equipment we had that we were indeed speaking with Mary Lucille Myers.

There's a long-standing theory in the paranormal field that entities are unaware of their own deaths. It's also considered disrespectful and potentially harmful to remind the entity of their passing; investigators should instead focus on other aspects of their lives. As reluctant as we were to bring up the topic of Mary's suicide, we wanted to test this theory to see if Mary was aware of what happened to her.

We asked if she was experiencing any troubles at home. Our motion detector was set off. As the light grew dim, we asked if she could walk us through what happened on March 25, and if she recalled attempting to ingest cyanide. Nothing. We apologized for asking the question and if it was too personal, we apologized for offending her.

The air was still, and our devices weren't registering any environmental changes or signs of activity. After posing that question, the feeling in the room changed considerably. After again saying sorry to who we believed was Mary and reassuring her that it wasn't our intention to offend her, we asked if there was anyone else other than the surgical nurse present in the room.

The motion detector lit up and then the light dimmed. We asked if it was still Mary we were speaking to, and there was no response on our motion detector. We asked if there was someone else we were communicating with at that point and the motion detector flashed yet again.

> **Mustafa:** What spurred this line of questioning was an interesting bit of information Brandon shared with me when we first learned we'd investigate a hospital. He

said all of the hospitals he'd ever investigated that had activity seemed to have several entities in them. And oftentimes there was a chief entity that was a bully or ringleader of sorts. It's a difficult concept to wrap one's head around, but it seemed to account for the strange shift in tone.

We asked if there were others present and if this entity was speaking for them. The motion detector's light went off on both occasions.

The feeling in the room went from being light and brimming with positive emotion, to one that was tense and ominous. We believed we saw shadow movement at the end of the hall, but ultimately stood our ground given our success in securing intelligent responses on not one, but two devices in this area.

Even after seeing what we thought was a person at the end of the hallway, we stayed put and asked, "Are there other people here that you're not allowing to speak with us?" The motion detector went off. We asked if they heard the noise we made on the first floor, and the familiar blue light emanated again. We asked if they were upset by the fact that people were moving into the hospital. The blue light turned on. We encouraged any other entities to speak up if they chose to do so, and told them there would be changes made to the hospital whether anyone present welcomed them or not.

That's when our communication ended that night for good.

Attempts to continue our discussion with Mary halted for the rest of the investigation. Morning was fast approaching and we had more than our fair share of evidence to review. While what we experienced in the moment was astounding, we had no clue what remarkable evidence was waiting for us on the ambisonic microphone.

While we'd found some potentially compelling bits of evidence throughout the case, a strange aberration on a FLIR thermal imaging camera could most directly be attributed to a quick movement of someone's hand over the lens. Surprisingly we didn't capture any more visual phenomena on top of the body cam footage we gathered on night one.

During our back and forth question and answer sessions on the Data Logger and motion detector, the ambisonic microphone had recorded several EVPs that sounded like a woman's voice. But the most telling and undeniable of them occurred when we asked Mary to step away from the motion detector. Right after our request, we heard a woman say, "Oh, sorry." Immediately after that, the motion detector's light begins to dim.

The Other End of the Country

Mustafa: The tone of her "sorry" isn't one I'll ever forget. It was a familiar, polite, cautious tremble. The same way I'd apologize as a young man when visiting people for the first time, being careful not to offend anyone. Mary's story, combined with our investigation, resonated with me so much that I couldn't sleep. When our camera crew was shooting B-roll the following day, I entered Worley Hospital with other members of the team. I wanted to apologize to Mary for bringing up the suicide and let her know that she was more than welcome there; the hospital's owners wanted her to stay if she felt comfortable. After asking if she understood several times, I didn't receive any hits on my Data Logger, save for two pressure changes. Gone was the dark and ominous feeling of the previous night's investigation, however. I had no choice but to feel content to leave. I would love to revisit the hospital someday to further investigate it.

Something that didn't appear in the aired episode was while we were taking a break outside, several members of the team and crew, myself included, saw someone peering outside from the window. It appeared to be the round face of a woman. Some team members went inside, one of them female. One by one, people took turns peering out the window to try and re-create the sighting. It was the female team member's face that most closely resembled the countenance we swore had looked directly at us as we discussed the next phases of the investigation.

Fast forward to a month later. I was with the team in Manhattan on a yacht fulfilling a media promotion for the re-launch of the show. While sitting on the boat after talking with several journalists and media personalities, my phone buzzed. I opened my notifications and saw texts from producer Kaylen Hadley who had worked the case with us in Pampa. She had managed to find photographs of Mary Lucille Myers after speaking with an employee at a local high school. The employee tried to locate Mary's graduation photos but came up short. However, something told her to keep looking. In an unmarked box, sandwiched between a stack of documents and photos, was a solitary picture of a smiling, round-faced nurse standing above a patient in a wheelchair. Written on the photograph was the name Mary Lucille Stayton. By pure coincidence, we were able to find a picture of the young woman who resembled the face we saw in the window.

Like the fate of Worley Hospital, Mary's story is one of condemnation. Her young life held an auspicious future that was ultimately shattered and ended much too soon. If she felt guilt or regret for her actions, it was difficult to not want to allay it. If it was her we talked to, we hope that we did. We can't help but wonder that if Mary had lived, would she have taken a lesson from the prospectors who'd seen Pampa's wells dry up? Would she have sought out other abundant fields to mine? Could she have persisted long enough to see the smiling woman in that photograph as someone who accomplished so much at such a young age? Could she have created a new life where her condemnation was a source of strength? It's a much happier thought than picturing her desolate, walking the soiled halls of Worley, peering out of boarded-up windows at cracked, dusty streets in a town once so full of life and promise, longing for better days.

Our Conclusion

Brandon: In my years of research, one thing is clear: not all hauntings are the same. Some cases can be very emotional and make you feel a serious human connection to the phenomena taking place. This was definitely the case for Worley Hospital. It's not often we can cross-classify a haunting. Because of the emotional connection and unfortunate suicide of Mary, we can classify this haunting as a Class One: Guilt-Ridden Entity crossed with a Class Three: Suicide Apparition. This case was not only complex with a serious breakthrough, but it is also a case that will stick with me for the rest of my life.

CONCLUSION

After sixteen years of paranormal research, we are just scratching the surface of the classification system. We have had the honor to work with some of the most intelligent people from various technical industries. With their guidance, you have been given a look into our theories, ethics, standards, and protocol that have laid the foundation for our classification system. We hope this book can be the foundation for all paranormal investigators that are looking to advance the field from a scientific perspective.

As our research of ghosts and hauntings continues, the classification system will evolve and grow. It is our honor and pleasure to help this field step out of the shadow of pseudoscience. Let this book aid you in your search for answers in the final frontier: the existence of life after death.

BIBLIOGRAPHY

"Black Holes," NASA Science, https://science.nasa.gov/astrophysics/focus-areas/black-holes.

Briscoe, Tony. "The massive glacier that formed the Great Lakes is disappearing—and greenhouse gases are to blame for its untimely demise." *Chicago Tribune.* February 28, 2019. https://www.chicagotribune.com/news/ct-met-disappearing-glacier-great-lakes-20190213-story.html.

Brown, Dee. *Bury My Heart at Wounded Knee.* 1970.

Cheung, Theresa. *The Element Encyclopedia of Ghosts and Hauntings: The Ultimate A-Z of Spirits, Mysteries and the Paranormal.* Harper Element, 2010.

"CPI Inflation Calculator," U.S. Bureau of Labor Statistics, https://www.bls.gov/data/inflation_calculator.htm.

Crowley, Aleister, and S.L. MacGregor Mathers. *The Lesser Key of Solomon.* 1904.

Denning, Hazel M. *True Hauntings: Spirits with a Purpose.* St. Paul: Llewellyn Publications, 1996.

DNR.MO.GOV, National Register of Historic Places Inventory Nomination Form, 1978, 1979.

"Ely Parker: Iroquois Chief and Union Officer," HistoryNet, 2021. https://www.historynet.com/ely-parker-iroquois-chief-and-union-officer.htm.

"Haunted Hotel." @GhostHunters. Instagram. September 26, 2019.

Hawthorne, Nathaniel. *The House of the Seven Gables.* 1851, Chapter 1. https://www.cliffsnotes.com/literature/h/the-house-of-the-seven-gables/summary-and-analysis/chapter-1/chapter-1-4.

"History of Cape Girardeau." City of Cape Girardeau. 2018. https://www.cityofcapegirardeau.org/about/history.

"Hospital for Roustabouts." Newspapers.com, 1854.

Kobrowski, Nicole R. "Dr. Helene Knabe: Revictimized in Death." Indiana History Blog. July 30, 2018. https://blog.history.in.gov/dr-knabe-revictimized-in-death/.

———. *She Sleeps Well.* Westfield, Indiana: Unseenpress.com, 2016.

Lane, Eloise. "The Legacy of Phebe Worley." White Deer Land Museum. Excerpt from the story of Earnest and Amanda Reynolds in Gray County Heritage FOCUS. Summer 1992, p. 13. https://pampamuseum.org/phebe-worley/.

Lavoisier, Antoine. "The Conservation of Mass Energy." Chem Team. https://www.chemteam.info/Equations/Conserv-of-Mass.html.

Lovecraft, H.P. *The History of the Necronomicon.* 1938.

"The Madison Home: From a Grand Army to Ghosts." Ohio
    Memory. April 13, 2018. https://ohiomemory.ohiohistory
    .org/archives/3768.

Martin, Sean. "Black holes may be the key to time travel and make
    'billions of years pass in minutes.'" *Express UK*. May 24, 2020.
    https://www.express.co.uk/news/science/1178555/black
    -hole-time-travel-time-dilation-how-to-time-travel-possible
    -black-hole-earth.

"Morrill Act," Ourdocuments.gov. https://www.ourdocuments
    .gov/doc.php?flash=false&doc=33.

Palinsky, Debbie. "History of the Ohio Cottage building." *Star
    Beacon*. October 31, 2009. https://www.starbeacon.com
    /archives/history-of-the-ohio-cottage-building/article
    _164fcb1d-287b-5959-ba0c-1123a67eb73f.html.

Peach, Emily. *Things That Go Bump in The Night: How to Investigate
    and Challenge Ghostly Experiences.* Thorsons Pub, 1991.

Redd, Nola Taylor. "Einstein's Theory of General Relativity."
    Space.com. November 7, 2017. https://www.space.com
    /17661-theory-general-relativity.html.

Ricarte, Angelo. "A Link between Ram Pressure Stripping and
    Active Galactic Nuclei." *Astrophysical Journal Letters* 895, no. 1
    (2020).

Rogan, Joe. "1216: Sir Roger Penrose." *The Joe Rogan Experience.*
    December 18, 2018. Podcast on Podchaser, https://www
    .podchaser.com/podcasts/the-joe-rogan-experience-10829
    /episodes/1216-sir-roger-penrose-34876792.

Scorsese, Martin, dir. *The Departed*. 2006; New York: Warner Brothers, 2007. DVD.

Shelton, Jim. "Under pressure, black holes feast." YaleNews. May 22, 2020. https://news.yale.edu/2020/05/22/under-pressure-black-holes-feast.

Smith, Robert W., and Dorothy A. Nicholson. "VONNEGUT AND BOHN ARCHITECTURAL RENDERINGS, 1896, 1911." Indiana History. December 2007. https://indianahistory.org/wp-content/uploads/vonnegut-and-bohn-architectural-renderings-1896.pdf.

Spitzer, Kirk, Yokkaichi. "The American POWs Still Waiting for an Apology From Japan 70 Years Later." *TIME*. September 12, 2014. https://time.com/3334677/pow-world-war-two-usa-japan/.

"Steamer Grey Eagle Is Wrecked." Iowa History Project. May 9, 1861. http://iagenweb.org/history/rivers/greyeaglewreck.htm.

Taylor, Troy. "The Original Springs Hotel in Okawville, Illinois." Haunted Illinois. 2004. https://www.hauntedillinois.com/realhauntedplaces/original-springs-hotel.php.

Thorne, Kip S. *Black Holes and Time Warps*. New York: W. W. Norton & Company, 1994.

The Washington Union. January 3, 1857. newspapers.com.

Wilson, Lindsey. "Why Do Broadway Theatres Keep a 'Ghost Light' Burning on the Stage?" Playbill. September 19, 2008. https://www.playbill.com/article/ask-playbillcom-the-ghost-light-com-153440.

"Worley Hospital Faces Closure, Opened in 1928." *Pampa Daily News*, September 5, 1975.

Zarrelli, Natalie. "How the Hidden Sounds of Horror Movie Soundtracks Freak You Out." Atlas Obscura. October 31, 2016. https://www.atlasobscura.com/articles/how-the-hidden -sounds-of-horror-movie-soundtracks-freak-you-out.

To Write to the Author

If you wish to contact the author or would like more information about this book, please write to the author in care of Llewellyn Worldwide Ltd. and we will forward your request. Both the author and the publisher appreciate hearing from you and learning of your enjoyment of this book and how it has helped you. Llewellyn Worldwide Ltd. cannot guarantee that every letter written to the author can be answered, but all will be forwarded. Please write to:

Brandon Alvis
Mustafa Gatollari
% Llewellyn Worldwide
2143 Wooddale Drive
Woodbury, MN 55125-2989

Please enclose a self-addressed stamped envelope for reply,
or $1.00 to cover costs. If outside the U.S.A., enclose
an international postal reply coupon.

Many of Llewellyn's authors have websites with additional information and resources. For more information, please visit our website at http://www.llewellyn.com.